RURAL IDENTITIES

For Brock

Rural Identities
Ethnicity and Community
in the Contemporary English Countryside

SARAH NEAL
Open University, UK

ASHGATE

Published by
Ashgate Publishing Limited
Wey Court East
Union Road
Farnham
Surrey, GU9 7PT
England

Ashgate Publishing Company
Suite 420
101 Cherry Street
Burlington
VT 05401-4405
USA

www.ashgate.com

British Library Cataloguing in Publication Data
Neal, Sarah
    Rural identities : ethnicity and community in the
    contemporary English countryside
    1. Sociology, Rural - England 2. Ethnicity - England
    3. National characteristics, English
    I. Title
    307.7'2'0942

Library of Congress Cataloging-in-Publication Data
Neal, Sarah.
    Rural identities : ethnicity and community in the contemporary English
countryside / by Sarah Neal.
        p. cm.
    Includes bibliographical references and index.
        ISBN 978-0-7546-7306-4 -- ISBN 978-0-7546-9143-3 (ebook) 1.
England--Rural conditions. 2. Ethnicity--England. 3. Community
development--England. 4. National characteristics, English. I. Title.

    HN385.5.N45 2009
    307.72089'00941--dc22

                                                                2009002151

ISBN   978 0 7546 7306 4
eISBN   978 0 7546 9143 3 (ebook)

Mixed Sources
Product group from well-managed
forests and other controlled sources
www.fsc.org Cert no. SGS-COC-2482
© 1996 Forest Stewardship Council

Printed and bound in Great Britain by
TJ International Ltd, Padstow, Cornwall

Contents

List of Figures and Tables

Figure

Tables

Acknowledgements

A book is never just the product of the person who wrote it of course. It emerges from and is part of a dialogue with an existing body of research and scholarship and this book is no different. It also involves a range of people and organisations who have all shared a relationship to it and to who I am deeply indebted. Perhaps the best place to start would be to thank those participants in the research project – on which much of this book is based – who gave so generously of their time and were willing to share their often intimate thoughts and experiences about living in the countryside. I want to extend my thanks to The Leverhulme Trust who funded the project and whose support of academic research is so important. I am always grateful to Sue Walters, the project's ever capable and always committed Research Fellow. She cannot be thanked enough for her fine fieldwork abilities and for her friendship.

I am endlessly appreciative of my colleagues who are, by some good fortune and rather wonderfully, also my friends (mainly but not only) at the Open University. Individually and collectively, they offer me new, demanding and enriching ideas and manage to effortlessly combine doing this with being caring, supportive and fun. In no order I would like to thank John Clarke, John Solomos, Vron Ware, Julian Agyeman, Eugene McLaughlin, Janet Newman, Gail Lewis, Esther Saraga, Gerry Mooney, Carol Vincent and Brian Linnekar for their many contributions to my thinking through the various permeations of rurality, nation, ethnicity and identity. However, it is Allan Cochrane, who read and commented so indispensably on drafts of chapters, who doesn't let me forget about the urban, who provides endless encouragement and who always gives me inspiration (despite his doubts about country music), who is owed an especial and very heartfelt thanks. He knows how important he is to me. Needless to say none of these people bear any responsibility for the content of the book and its various muddles and misunderstandings.

Caroline Wintersgill, Neil Jordan and Emily Jarvis at Ashgate must be thanked for their initial receptiveness to the idea of the book and for their support and (much tried) patience in realising it.

And then of course there are my family and friends who travel with me always. They do so (mostly) without complaint and with forbearance. They indeed need to be thanked – they are much treasured.

This book is dedicated to Brock.

Chapter 1

Introduction

I want to begin with two narrations.

The first comes from a colleague of mine, Esra, at the Open University. I was talking to her about writing this book and explaining how I had been thinking a lot about the natural and the social and the ways in which these connected to my research and the project. As we were talking Esra, who had migrated from Turkey to Germany with her family when she was a little girl, told me how at her first school in Germany the class had been set a nature quiz – naming native trees and flowers. It is the sort of quiz many of us may recall doing at school. I have clear memories of trying to carefully trace around leaves and writing the names of trees next to these efforts. Esra told me about how difficult she found the naming of German plants and how she only got very low marks and how this experience emphasised her 'newness' to the nation. And while she is sure now that there were other children in the class who also did badly in the quiz, for Esra her struggle to successfully identify German trees and plants – German nature – was felt as a 'jolt' moment, a moment in which she experienced her migrant status and her non-belonging to the nation.

The second comes from the murder of the South London teenager Stephen Lawrence in 1993 and the witness statements of Conor and Louise Taaffe who were leaving their church near the bus stop immediately after the attack on Stephen. Although initially frightened they went to Stephen's aid and realising how badly he was injured held him and tried to comfort him telling him how much he was loved by his family and that help was on its way. When they returned to their home afterwards they had Stephen's blood on their hands. They washed their hands into a container and went into their garden and carefully poured the water mixed with blood onto a rose bush they had. Reading or hearing this witness account is poignant. The description of this instinctive and ceremonial 'small act' of going to the rose bush is deeply moving and it seems to capture the proximity of nature to social behaviours and the ways in which nature and non-human things are deeply entangled within human emotions – not least those emotions that anyone hearing of this witness account feel themselves.

These very different narrations both open up some of the questions and the puzzles with which this book engages:

- What happens to the concepts with which this book is concerned – the countryside, ethnicity, community (and their relationality) – if they are viewed through a notion of the convergence between the categories 'the natural' and 'the social'?
- To what extent does rural nature exclude or become mobilised in order to deny social inclusion?
- Conversely to what extent can nature transcend social divisions and open up routes of belonging and attachment?
- How do people use and interact with the non-human in intimate and emotional discourses and practices?

Why Countryside, Community and Ethnicity?

In many ways I began worrying at these questions and puzzles in earlier work (see for example Neal, 2002; Neal and Walters, 2005, 2006, 2007; Neal and Agyeman, 2006) in which I examined and challenged the ways in which rural landscapes become sometimes implicitly and sometimes explicitly whitened geographical territories sustaining particular fantasies of nation. Julian Agyeman and I concluded our edited collection by arguing for what we called more 'broken narratives of the rural'. By this we meant that the turbulence of the countryside needed to be accounted for – that the countryside needed to be more widely acknowledged as an uncertain landscape, as a site of social struggle and cultural and economic heterogeneity and, directly related to this heterogeneity, as an unsettled and in flux space which has very different meanings attached to it beyond those of 'rural idyll' and a 'rural crisis'; as a space in which the idea of a black and minority ethnic presence and engagement is unremarkable and normative and a black and minority ethnic rural absence remarkable and strange. In short Julian and I concurred with a number of rural scholars (Cloke and Little, 1997, Sibley, 1995; Halfacree, 1997; 2007) when we argued for richer, multiple narratives of rurality in contemporary Britain (2006: 242).

Since this advocation for broken narratives of rurality there has been a little flurry of books (for example, Benson, 2005; Askwith, 2007; Kingsnorth, 2007) and media debate (for example *The Independent*, 9 September 2005; 31 March 2008) about the meaning of Englishness and the state of the English rural in particular. At the heart of these books and media deliberations are expressions of anxiety as to a vanishing countryside and with it a vanishing Englishness. While this anxiety is by no means a new one – as Raymond Williams (1979) observed three decades ago the worry of a golden rurality that has, or is about to irrevocably disappear is a constant presence (see also Neal and Agyeman, 2006) – the timing and the cluster of voices raised around this is noteworthy for a number of reasons. These debates come at a time when, intensified by the continual background and not so background white noise of a 'crisis of multiculturalism' (Lewis and Neal, 2005;

McLaughlin and Neal, 2007) and by the partial and (potentially full) devolution of Wales and Scotland, Britishness and Englishness and their dominant political position and meanings are increasingly uncertain and fragile. That the worries about the countryside should be written into these anxieties about nation reinforce the long relation between countryside and country. In other words the countryside is a mirror. That the countryside should itself be viewed as being in crisis is a reflection of the (seeming) crisis of English identity.

This co-joined relationship captured in Roger Askwith's (2007) book revealingly titled *The Lost Village: In Search of a Forgotten Rural England.* Askwith begins by returning home to the Northamptonshire village where he lives after a year being abroad. Sitting at an Remembrance Day service in the village church he recalls lines from Philip Larkin 'I thought it would last my time/The sense that, beyond town,/There would always be fields and farms,/Where the village louts could climb/Such trees as were not cut down.' Askwith then remembers the further lines from the same poem 'For the first time I feel somehow/That it isn't going to last...' and he goes on to explain how,

> the truth of Larkin's words had suddenly struck me. It – this village – wasn't going to last [...] the actual village – that miniature, self-contained eco system in which past and present were all tangled up, and people, buildings and vegetation shared on reasonably coherent collective story – that village had passed away long ago [...] Perhaps I had assumed that, somewhere in the background of my life there would always be, not just one village, but a whole network of many thousand villages, each with its own story and its own local families and its own unique landscape and memories and its own peculiar way of saying and doing things. In short I had imagined a rural England and had blithely gone through life (eagerly embracing the modern wherever I found it) under the impression that it would always be there, like a great rock, with the past clinging to it like lichen. Now when I turned to look at it, *it was gone.* (2007: 6–7. Emphasis added)

Real England (2007) is Paul Kingsnorth's indictment of contemporary England and what he sees as the erosion of English culture and identity by bland corporatism and the endless advance of global market forces. While explaining that he comes 'from a family with an urban history' and has 'never been part of the land' (2007: 161) Kingsnorth, like Roger Asquith and Roger Scruton (2000) a little earlier, argues that there is a loss of rural culture in England and that he 'can feel its heartbreaking power'. For example, in one of the chapters in his book Kingsnorth describes spending time with various local people in three villages in England. Walking with his guide in Barton, Cambridgeshire through fields and along streams looking for butterflies and bee orchids and seeing poppies, yellow rattles, hares and fox cubs Kingsnorth comments, it is genuinely hard for someone of my generation to imagine that much of the English countryside was like this just fifty years ago. I almost wish I hadn't seen it. If you don't know what you've lost, it doesn't hurt. But I'm glad I wasn't around to se the loss of places like this on a national scale. It would have been hard to take. As a nation our mental image of rural England is still composed of places like this. Hay meadows, gambolling lambs, poppy fields, spinneys. A curious, almost childlike country landscape: part Beatrix Potter, part Rupert Bear. We don't know or don't want to know *how broken it is*. (Ibid.: 157. Emphasis added)

I have quoted at some length from *The Lost Village* and *Real England* because they both capture an anxious melancholy about social change. They speak of things vanishing or broken and in doing so both Askwith and Kingsnorth invoke the constant proximity of rural-nation relation. Within this argument the changing, endangered countryside is always, and at the same time, the changing, endangered nation. In this way I would suggest that debates and deliberations about the countryside are inevitably debates and deliberations about ethnicity and identity. This is a theme that runs through this book.

This is not to deny that the social changes in rural areas that Askwith, Kingsnorth, Scruton and others are commenting on are not and have not taken place. The fundamental shifts in agricultural production that have taken place and impacted on the countryside in England and the wider UK are starkly apparent in even the briefest glances at the statistics. For example Benson (2005: 228–9) notes that 'in 1939 there were 500,000 farms in Britain...the majority of these were small mixed units of less than 50 acres...There are now 191,000 farms left and of those 19,000 account for more than 50 per cent of national output. It is estimated that three out of four jobs in British agriculture have been lost since 1945.' The extent to which the countryside has undergone systematic processes of economic restructuring is reflected in the shift from the 1950s when 'over a third (34.6 per cent) of the "rural population" of Britain was estimated to be dependent in agriculture for its income. By 1970 the proportion had fallen to 24.3 per cent, by 1990 to 19.6 per cent and by 2000 to 16.8 per cent' (Woods, 2005: 15). The most recent figures show a continued and rapid decline in the agricultural base of rural economies – according to the Commission for Rural Communities (2008: 2) 'agriculture accounts for no more than 2.8% of employment in rural areas'.

There is of course a recursiveness to these changes of which these economic shifts are an interactive part. Counter urbanisation and the flow of urban to rural migrants reflects, in part, imagined rural idylls and to be in those and imagined intact communities and the security of those. Of course counter urbanisation impacts on and contributes to changing those very rural spaces and communities that it simultaneously seeks out. So this book does not deny that the countryside is undergoing processes of change and restructuring. Rather it argues that the focus on the countryside and the shifts within it have fed into the establishment of two increasingly hegemonic but seemingly completely contradictory rural imaginings – one of idyll and one of crisis.

Table 1.1   Two versions of the contemporary English countryside

Rural idyll	Rural crisis
	Break down of communities
Intact communities	House prices and housing shortages
A sense of community	Closure of shops and social amenities
Safety and security	A lack of neighbourliness and an absence
Neighbourliness and social care	of social care
Small scale and local agricultural economies	Rural restructuring and the rise of agri-business
Open spaces	Commuting
Privacy and solitude	Isolation
Proximity to nature and rural traditions	Attacks and restrictions on rural practices
Reaffirming Englishness and cultural security	and traditions
	Loss of national identity and cultural insecurity
Timelessness	
	Constant change

What setting out the key features of each version of the countryside does is emphasise their connectedness rather than their separateness. While the idyll and crisis positions would appear to work in parallel to the other they of continually bump into, collide with and co-constitute each other. It is notions of community and ethnic identity that in particular work as the socially based drivers in these co-joined discourses but these are also bound by and interact with notions of nature. At one level this is a very obvious point to make. After all the spatial context and scrutinised subject is 'the social relations of the countryside' and the countryside *is* all about real and imagined forms of 'rural nature'. But surprisingly, in many of the debates about rural spaces, their contestations and the processes and practices of social inclusion and exclusion, rural nature itself is often uncommented on, taken as a given or seems like the hovering, slightly awkward, forgotten guest at the party (see Bell and Newby, 1979; Cohen, 1982; Milbourne, 1994; Chakraborti and Garland, 2004 for example). This splitting between the social and non-human worlds produces a the focus on the former with the latter providing the mere context in which the dramas of the social are carried out and can be read as reflective of modernist tendencies to discount, diminish, manage and control nature. In his examination of the relationship between emotions, geography and nature Mark Smith quotes Luc Ferry's (1995: xvi) assertion that 'nature is a dead letter for us. Literally it no longer speaks to us for we have long ceased – at least since Descartes – to attribute a soul to it or believe it inhabited by occult forces'. Smith counters 'contra Ferry, I will argue, nature is a dead-letter only to those "moderns" who have lost the ability to listen to and interpret the non-human world' (2005: 222).

What the Askwith and Kingsnorth texts do is engage with rural nature. It may be a rather instrumental engagement when they incorporate the non-human and rural nature directly into their worries about all that is being lost and damaged within their rural/national crisis discourse but nevertheless nature has a clear presence. Using the narratives I began with in this chapter is also an attempt to emphasise how the non-human and rural nature both write and get written into experiences of exclusion; of empathy and of care for others. What seems important to me is to ask so what happens when nature very directly writes and gets written into examinations of the countryside, of community, of ethnicity and of identity? Of concern is how and at what moments rural nature is enrolled, drawn on and invested in social meaning making and everyday social practices.

In many ways I follow here in the steps of Michael Bell (1993) and his ethnographic study of the Hampshire village of Childerley in the late 1980s. What is of concern to Bell is the what he calls the 'social experience of nature' (ibid.: 4) and the ways in which the inhabitants of Childerley constructed their social identities as 'country people' *through* nature (ibid.: 6). In the time he spent living in the village and talking to residents it was rural nature that was the theme and topic that was continually returned to and discussed and the filter through which social relations were analysed and the agonistic dimensions of these reconciled (see Chapters 3 and 6). In the study that I undertook with Sue Walters – the study with which this book engages – we found very similar entanglements of the social and the natural at work in terms of allowing the people we spoke to, to make sense of the local, national and global worlds in which they lived their lives. This brought to mind the way in which Richard Mabey argues in *Nature Cure* that 'we constantly refer back to the natural world to try and discover who we are. Nature is the most potent source of metaphors to describe and explain our behaviour and feelings' (2006: 19). Mabey also cites Ted Hughes' poem *The Swifts* and its lines 'The swifts are back – they've made it again' as symbols that humans use for reassurance – not only of the return of summer but more profoundly, that 'the globe's still working' (ibid.: Hughes, 1982: 146–7). The social use and interaction with rural nature in relation to the countryside, to identity formations around both ethnicity and community began to be of increasing intrigue to me during the 'doing of' the research project on which much of this book is based. Letting rural nature *in* – into my attempts to think about the findings from the project and to working out what those findings offered in relation to understanding the social, community, the countryside and to questions of belonging and inclusion in rural spaces is a connective thread that runs through this book. Another connective thread is the use of evidence drawn from the research project. It is this project that I now explain.

The Project

In 1992 Chris Philo urged rural geographers to rethink the relationship between the rural and its marginalised, subordinated and invisibilised others. The debate that followed has been a key shaper in the theoretical and empirical directions of rural studies over the 1990s and 2000s (Cloke and Little, 1997). In their response to Philo Jonathan Murdoch and Andy Pratt (1994: 85) warned against any simplistic re focusing of the analytical gaze on 'hidden others' in rural spaces and posed the question 'should we not attempt to reveal the ways of the powerful, exploring the means by which they make and sustain their domination?' With this debate in mind I have been concerned with examining the nature of the relationship between the contemporary English countryside and what I have described as the 'rurally included'. I use this term to describe those rural populations who can appear to make a confident, dominant and a seemingly uncontested claim to rural belonging. My interest was in the qualitative excavation of the co-ordinates that make up this relationship: what were these co-ordinates and in what ways are these narrated? What are the tensions and nuances that mark, bind and fracture the category of the 'included'? How, in what ways and in what spaces do senses of ethnicity, Englishness and nation enter and shape these processes?

At the heart of the project were three concerns. First, the ways in which the English countryside can be assembled as a cultural and social space in which particular versions of majority–ethnicised belonging are reproduced and reinforced. Second, the ways in which recent high levels of urban to rural migration and socio-economic changes in the countryside have (re)shaped contemporary rural social relations. The third concern was to access everyday articulations and practices of belonging, commonality, difference and place by members of local rural communities in the English countryside. The connection between these concerns and the category of the 'rurally included' has occurred through a focus on two rural social organisations that are very much associated with the countryside – the National Federation of Women's Institutes (NFWI) and the National Federation of Young Farmers Clubs (NFYFC). These two organisations have significant differences in their membership particularly in relation to generation and gender. Older women tend to constitute the commonest profile of Women's Institute (WI) membership. Members of Young Farmers' Clubs (YFC) are aged between 10–24. The Clubs attract a gender mix and include young people who may have only indirect agricultural connections. However, both Women's Institutes and Young Farmers' Clubs contain a number of similarities: they are *the* social organisations most heavily associated with mainstream English rural culture; they are both intensely local but also have national profiles and while they are both leisure organisations, they both carry a sense of community responsibility, of being at the heart of rural well-being and of rural policy development.

In gaining access to the people who participated in the project through their involvement in these organisations the project did not make any claims to be researching a *representative* sample of rural populations. My intention was clearly *not* to access such a sample but rather to reach a very *particular* rural constituency that was neither representative nor was it one that sought to access marginalised or other rural populations. What the project sought to reach and try to capture were normative and 'mainstreamed' rural voices. What the project has addressed is the relationality between rurality, Englishness and identity but without making any direct reference to otherness and difference and yet in doing so it sought to shed light on how processes of social inclusion and being 'accounted for' may still work through anxieties about and perceptions and senses of others and external threats.

The focus on the National Federation of Women's Institutes and the National Federation of Young Farmers Clubs allowed an examination of two organisations that have a high profile association with the rural and, particularly with the NFWI, an association with Englishness. In her historical analysis of the Women's Institute movement and its relationship with feminist politics Andrews (1997) notes that between 1915 and 1960, 'for women in the NFWI their ruralism enabled them to be included in definitions of the nation and indeed at times to be perceived as the *epitome of Englishness*' (1997: 42. Emphasis added). This rural-nation connection has not shifted significantly. For example, after addressing the General Assembly meeting of the National Federation of Women's Institutes in 2000 the then Prime Minister, Tony Blair, was famously slow handclapped and the event was widely covered in the media with the members of the National Federation being variously described as 'the backbone of middle England' (*Daily Mail*, 8 June 2000), the *Mirror* (8 June 2000) as 'Mrs England' and the *Guardian* as 'middle Britain respectability'.

The Women's Institute is then perhaps the best-known rural organisation. The first institute was established in North Wales in 1915 and the NFWI was and remains the largest social, and women's, organisation in England and Wales (www. womensinstitute.org.uk). Today the NFWI has a quarter of a million members spread across 8,000 locally/village based institutes that are themselves organised into 70 county and island federations in England and Wales. The National Executive and Head Office is in London. The membership base is heavily clustered in the 50–65 age range and has far fewer young women members. The membership base has no profile on ethnicity. *Home and Country* is the NFWI's monthly magazine.

Like the NFWI the NFYFC is an old organisation. It was established in Devon in 1931 and it also has an extensive structure and a significant, although smaller, membership. There are 700 Young Farmers Clubs existing in England and Wales. These are grouped into 49 federations which themselves are organised into six regional areas in England (www.nfyfc.org.uk). The organisation has approximately 20,000–25,000 members in these locally based clubs and members range from 10–26 years old. The National Executive and Head Office is based in the National Agriculture Centre in Warwickshire. The organisation has a quarterly magazine, *Ten26*. As with the NFWI the NFYFC have a particular association with gender although for the NFYFC this is a masculine association. This is somewhat misleading as the NFYFC has an estimated 50/50 gender balance and, reflecting the changing nature of rural communities, at least 50 per cent of NFYFC members no longer have any connection to agriculture.

As I noted earlier the NFWI and the NFYFC see themselves as playing a central community role. This has been re-emphasised in the context of rural change as this statement from the then Chair of the Women's Institute Federation in Devon makes clear, 'Membership of the WI is about giving to the community. It is also about friendship, education and helping each other. In many ways, as rural post offices have closed and the church has withdrawn, *it is the WI that holds the community together*' (*Daily Mail*, 10 June 2000. Emphasis added). The NFYFC similarly sees itself occupying a key position for promoting community values. For example their home page introductory statement states 'the ideal of citizenship is fundamental to YFC and is provided by creating an awareness of community responsibility' (www.nfycf.org.uk. Accessed 8 September 2005).

There is a plurality in the role of these rural social organisations; they are about leisure provision, but they are also about the construction of a rural community and a network of belonging. Being a member of the NFWI or the NFYFC involves 'being' in the village and/or the locality. In this way these rural social organisations can be seen as taking up interesting and possibly conflicting roles in local social worlds which then extend to the broader formative terrains of rural identities. For example, on the one hand they may be understood as sites of governance and regulation and/or 'defence' in which an English ethnicity and 'village values' are reproduced and reaffirmed. Or, on the other hand they may be understood as inclusive hubs which are open and alive to the changing constituents of contemporary rural worlds and which provide and enact practices of community and social care.

In order to access the local worlds of these organisations, the research project drew its sample from, and accessed members of local Women's Institutes and Young Farmers Clubs in, three diverse areas of rural England. It is clear from earlier research (Neal, 2002) that the English countryside cannot be conceived as a homogenous geographic, economic or social entity. Different areas of rural England vary extensively across these axis and, in recognition of this the project selected three county delineated geographical areas – Hertfordshire, North Devon and Northumberland – in which to approach local Young Farmers Clubs and Women's Institutes. Hertfordshire was selected because of its location at the edges of north London and its proximity to the metropolis and its consequent 'commuter belt' identity. Despite this, and a heavy concentration of motorway networks, Hertfordshire has remained 'an attractive pastoral and agricultural landscape' (*Municipal Year Book*, 2002: 503). In *Howard's End*, a novel set in Hertfordshire and centred on ideas of class and nation, E.M. Forster describes the county as 'England at its quietest, with little emphasis of river and hill; it is England meditative' (2000: 198). It is also a rural England that the Census (2002) survey reveals as an affluent and economically active region. It has a younger than national average population profile and although its minority ethnic population is lower than the national average Hertfordshire has a significant black and minority ethnic population (4.8 per cent). In contrast, North Devon was chosen because of its relationship to a dominant imagining of an 'authentic' English countryside, i.e. the classic 'chocolate box', thatched cottage, rural idyll. Because of this 'identity' North Devon is attractive to tourists and as a retirement destination. This is reflected in its higher end age profile and its lower levels of employment. The inclusion of Northumberland was a means of taking the project to the outer reaches of England with its remoteness from the South East and its geographical proximity to Scotland. The ethnicity profiles of both these regions do evidence the dominance of whiteness. The 2002 Census data shows 99 per cent of the North Devon population to be white and Northumberland to be between 99.3 and 99.8 per cent white. This is again reflected in the profile of focus group participants who were all white and mainly English. In terms of gender the participant profile of the focus groups differed according to whether they were WI or YFC based. The WI focus groups were completely female and were mainly in the 50+ age category. The YFC focus groups tended to be gender balanced and most group members were in the late adolescent to early twenties age category. A small number of the YFC focus groups did include younger participants. In total the project conducted 30 focus group interviews with local WI and YFCs in these case study areas.

Focus groups are increasingly used in academic research and they offer a number of advantages. Focus group interviews allow researchers access to group-based norms and dynamics and to the process of collectively produced social knowledges (May, 2001; Green and Hart, 1999). It is the very interactive character of focus group interviews that is valuable because it illuminates 'the comparisons that participants make among each other's experiences and opinions [which] are a valuable source of insights into complex behaviours and motivations' (Morgan, 1997: 15). Focus groups were envisaged as being particularly appropriate for the project because they offered a forum in which members would be surrounded by their friends and/or acquaintances and this would help facilitate the interactive discussion of topics that could be perceived as unfamiliar, emotive and complex (Farquhar, 1999: 47). Using focus groups also directly related to the ways in which both social organisations operate – WIs and YFCs meet as convivial groups on a regular, often weekly basis. In addition, the participation-led nature of focus groups means that they are less dominated by the researcher than would be the case in an individual interview setting. This was again important given that locality and collective conversations were central to the project. These were the advantages that were envisaged in the design of the project. The challenges and difficulties of focus group interviews emerged as the fieldwork was underway and I return to discuss these in Chapter 3 (see also Neal and Walters, 2005).

Access to the local clubs and institutes was negotiated through local WI and YFC organisers. Although establishing access was a laborious process, and complicated by the organisations' various committee structures, local WIs and YFCs were keen to take part in the project. A willingness to be involved in social research is often multi-motivated and the role of the researcher, who they are and what they say, is only one part of a complex set of reasons behind the willingness of people and/or organisations to become respondents. The one to two hour interview schedule was organised around a series of prompts (and pictures) which aimed to access perceptions and practices of rurality, locality and attachment; imaginings of Englishness, nation and belonging; experiences of local and national change and continuity in the countryside and views on the WI and YFC and their constituencies and roles in rural communities. While the sample groups most closely resemble the snowball method there was an element of spatial sampling as we wanted to select clubs and institutes that reflected the local geographies of each of the three areas. The data from these interviews was analysed through the 'constant comparison' method which enabled us to move from broad to more focused coding. This process was enhanced through the use of N6 software to store, code, retrieve and search the data set. It is important to note that the views and experiences expressed by the participants are theirs alone and do not represent any official position of either the WI or YFCs. It is also important to note that all the names of villages and focus group participants have been anonymised.

While I have addressed some of the methodological issues arising from the project elsewhere (Neal and Walters, 2005) I do consider aspects of the research relationship and the roles and positions that emerged between the researchers and the researched at various points in the chapters here as thinking through some of the methodological questions that arose for the project effectively illuminates some of the key knots of the wider relationship between the personal, rural identity, inclusion and belonging. It is the structure of the book and the focus of its chapters that I that now outline.

How the Book is Organised

Working across six substantive chapters the book begins in Chapter 2 by addressing why and how a series of contested concepts – rurality, ethnicity, community – powerfully and simultaneously intersect in the phrase 'the English countryside'. Suggesting that the English countryside has always been and continues to be a hybridised real and imagined space of highly diverse and competing demands, desires, anxieties, claims, commodifications and consumption the chapter is concerned with how this produces 'rural others' and processes of social and cultural exclusion within narratives of the rural and within narratives of the Englishness. Directly developing the themes begun here in the discussions of the relationality between country and countryside Chapter 2 focuses on the ways in which the categories of the countryside and of rurality have been analytically approached and conceptualised. In particular it explores the cultural turn in this analysis and the ways in which debates about rurality have become intensely contested debates about nation/al representations, social and economic change, social exclusion, social disadvantage, controversial legislation and regulation and so on. It is at the intersection between the rural as a place of apparent homogeneity, order and certainty and the rural as a place of heterogeneity, instability and uncertainty that Chapter 2 argues it is possible to view the increasing turbulence as to what the rural means and the shift, as Michael Woods (2005) has put it from 'rural politics' to the 'politics of the rural'.

Chapter 3 examines the enduring and renewed interest in, the phenomenon of the rural community. It tracks the ways in which this has been approached in geographical, anthropological and sociological studies of rural social relations in the UK. The chapter examines both the seductive appeal of and the troublesome nature of 'the rural community' and the ways in which it works as an inclusive narrative of local belonging despite the extent and depth of local social and economic cleavages. Chapter 3 suggests that while rural communities were always more heterogeneously constituted and conflictual than popularly supposed the desires for community, for the ontological securities which stem from this and for local connection in a globally perceived social world continue to sustain discourses and everyday practices of community-making, creating conviviality and providing informal networks of social care.

Chapter 4 is concerned with reviewing the concept of ethnicity and the ways in which locationality, non-human things and the corporeal are integral to processes of ethnic identification. The chapter suggests that there has been too little accounting of this in ethnicity debates. It asks what counts as markers of ethnic identity – exactly what gets assembled in order that ethnicity can be claimed/identified/practised/assigned and in particular how does this assemblage process work in relation to majoritised or normative ethnic identities? Using the metaphor of home and the examining the individual and collective aspects of ethnic formation the chapter suggests that, like community, ethnicity is also about searches and strategies for achieving ontological securities. While arguing for the need to look at non-human entities within ethnicity theory the chapter emphasises the need to not diminish the importance of the social.

Chapter 5 develops this argument through a focus on the entanglements of the relation between ethnically invested spaces and notions of community. It extends this discussion as to how structures of community feeling and ways of belonging are produced, maintained and re-created in everyday settings. Arguing that sociality is at the centre of the everyday experiences of community the chapter details the ways in which rural social organisations can be understood as taking up a particular and critical role in this process. Chapter 5 is concerned with investigating how notions and practices of conviviality, neighbourliness and kindness act as a particular kind of 'glue' in processes of community-making and maintenance. It considers the ways in which local social organisations such as the WI and YFCs appeal to, and speak for, particular rural constituents; it analyses the nature of their presence and work in rural communities through the concept of governance and scrutinises the extent (and limits) of these social organisations' social inclusiveness and on their flexibility to adapt to changing contemporary rural environments.

Chapter 6 extends the focus on practices of community-making but it uses the competing concepts of order, regulation and freedom and liberty to suggest that there are very divergent interpretations of rurality constantly at work even within dominant narratives of the countryside. The chapter is concerned to work through this paradox and suggests that the tensions and contradictions of the rural as orderly but also as anti-orderly are *partially* resolved through notions of who belongs and who can be included within rural communities. The stress on partial is important of course. If there is dissent with dominant narratives of the countryside and rural practices and values then it is possible to suggest from this basis that there may be possibilities for other dissenting voices and interpretations of 'what is the rural'. This is the thinking that is picked up on in Chapter 7.

Chapter 7 returns to the notion of ethnicity and the argument that it can be viewed as being assembled through composite mixes of the human and the non-human and suggests that this may work against the totalising and excluding tendencies of ethnic formation. Using actor-network theory (ANT) this chapter illustrates how participants invested both the non-human, 'natural' world (hills, trees, plants, rivers, weather, seasons) and the built environment (churches, cottages, village halls, manor houses, village greens) with national and local meanings subjectively shaped by attachment and familiarity. Chapter 7 argues that formations of dominant ethnic identity combine the non-human and the social as a way of naturalising and, by extension, securing ethnicity. However, the chapter emphasises the animating and multidimensional aspects of the non-human and the possibilities this presents for the non-human to be constantly re-read and counter claimed. In short Chapter 7 asks whether the non-human and its continual combining, relationality with the human mean there are routes – in this case through/within rural nature – for transformative belongings and attachments which may transcend processes of exclusion and social division. While it is with caution that Chapter 7 suggests possibilities of openness and transformative attachment what it does assert are the instabilities of ethnic formation and the hybrid, multidimensionality of rural spaces. It is this that forms the focus of the conclusions drawn in Chapter 8. These conclusions recursively address the ways in which the 'English rural' must be understood as a space that is relationally constituted; a space in which ontological security is sought and which it both offers and elides; a space that is subject to competing demands and interpretations; it is a liminal space which is in a process of constant becoming.

Chapter 2
Debating Rurality:
Englishness and Otherness

Introduction

In the previous chapter I suggested that anxieties about rural spaces are at the same time anxieties about the nation. This reflects the proximity and intimacy of the relationship between the English countryside and Englishness that I and others have commented on. This is not a new relationship of course (see Williams, 1979; Wright, 1984 for example) but its current intensity is significant. The rural idyll-rural crisis discourses that were discussed earlier can be understood as part of a series of wider, tangential but nevertheless connected discourses. For example, current debates that appear to be about the global, the nation/al and the urban – Britishness and UK devolution (Ware, 2007); post colonial melancholy (Gilroy, 2004); late modernity's ontological insecurities, individualism and senses of precariousness (Bauman, 1997; Young, 1999; 2007); the rapid urbanisation of the Global South, global corporate culture and environmental anxieties (Davis, 2005; Clarke, 2006; Cochrane and Talbot, 2008) can, as this chapter will set out to suggest, all be seen to be present in the pre-modern and post-modern simultaneous longings for, and worries about, rural spaces.

In this context my concerns here are to continue to think through why and how a series of contested concepts – rurality, ethnicity, community, nature – all potently intersect in the phrase 'the English countryside'. This thinking through process will suggest that more than anything these concepts work because they are able to complexly collapse a series of social inclusions and exclusions; the real and the imaginary; the material and the representational; social fears, reassurances and desires. Given this any efforts to try and make sense of the meanings and seemingly indomitable appeal of the term 'the English countryside' have to be prepared to both look at and then go beyond the more traditional definitions of the countryside which tended to rely solely on positivistic measurements of population size and types of local economic systems. The need to take a wider view of rurality requires an analysis that borrows from the cultural turn in geography which has meant a focus on notions of identity, and the spatial turn in sociology, which has allowed an explicit engagement between race and space. As David Goldberg puts it,

> The category of space is discursively produced and ordered. Just as spatial
> distinctions between 'East' and 'West' are racialised in their conception and

application, so racial categories have been variously spatialised more or less since their inception into continental divides, national localities and geographic regions. Racisms become institutionally normalised in and through spatial configuration, just as social space is made to seem natural, a given, by being conceived and defined in racial terms [...] after all, *social relations are not expressed in a spatial vacuum.* (1993: 185. Emphasis added)

Taking a wider view of rurality also needs to incorporate an emotional turn. To emotionalise the rural is recognise that countrysides are spaces of affect, eliciting (and demanding?) personal as well as public attachments, investments, enchantments, anxieties and ambivalences. This something that the work of the photographer Ingrid Pollard manages to very successfully capture (2004) and, as Ray Pahl importantly reminds us, 'people are not social atoms [...] people live in supportive personal communities that bind them both to places and people in subtle and complex ways' (2007: 15).

With these turns and emphases in mind this chapter performs three core tasks. First it traces the ways in which a critical, interdisciplinary rural studies literature – informed by such turns – has emerged, mainly in the UK context, since the early 1990s. Second it looks at those other figures and populations whose presence, rather than absence, in the English countryside troubles and/or unsettles dominant notions of rurality. Third the chapter attempts to show how these two concerns reflect and inflect a broader set of contemporary national and global anxieties.

Re-defining the Rural: The Critical Turn

As I noted in the previous chapter Chris Philo's (1992) call in the *Journal of Rural Studies* to rural studies scholars to rethink the meanings of and work done by the concept of rurality – what and who it mobilises and what and who it marginalises – has been influential in subsequent debates and social research (see for example Murdoch and Pratt, 1992; Philo, 1993; Cloke and Little, 1997). Philo's prompt to rural studies to look at what has been neglected and hidden in the research and analysis of rural spaces is now seen as an intervention that shifted rural studies away from positivistic interpretations and measurements of the countryside and the tendency to approach rural areas through quantitative, objective indicators and definitions such as population size, types of land use, agricultural economies and rural policy formations and delivery. Increasingly, rural studies have become preoccupied with the ways in which rural spaces are able to work as cultural metaphors, and are subjective and require qualitative approaches for understanding and analysing them.

This is not to suggest that 'older approaches' to the study of rural areas have been jettisoned or to argue that these and the quantitative methods they predominantly work with do not have a place within debates about the rural. They have not and they do. And certainly local and central rural policy-making and government interest still works very much within the positivistic parameters. For example the Rural Evidence Research Centre based at Birkbeck College (University of London) works extensively with the Department of Environment, Food and Rural Affairs (Defra) providing rurally relevant rural measurement tools, data sets and analysis of demographic and agricultural and social policy needs. It is the Rural Evidence Research Centre (RERC) which developed the 'Rural Definition' (2004) which central and local government and other policy organisations use to inform a range of rural and urban policy agendas. The Rural Definition replaced the previous and longstanding Tarling Definition developed in the Land Economy Department at Cambridge University in the 1970s. The Tarling definition, categorised rural and non-rural areas according to a local authorities' accessibility or remoteness – in other words, this definition posited that areas were rural or not depending on how close or distant they were to motorway and railway networks. In contrast to this remote/accessible binary definition of urban and rural areas the RERC Rural Definition uses a highly quantitative 'graded' measure of rurality based on what is described as a 'settlement-based approach'. It is a definition which is based purely on population sizes and patterns of dwelling and does not include any social and/or economic criteria. The grading system of the Rural Definition is able to spatially drill down below local authority levels and categorisations as it uses 'output areas' as its key units. These 'output areas' can be thought of as quantitative

Table 2.1   Summary of local authority rural and urban classifications

Classifications	Definitions
Major Urban	Districts with either 100,000 people or 50 per cent of their population in urban areas with a population of more than 750,000.
Large Urban	Districts with either 50,000 people or 50 per cent of their population in one of 17 urban areas with a population between 250,000 and 750,000.
Other Urban	Districts with fewer than 37,000 people or less than 26 per cent of their population in rural settlements and larger market towns.
Significant Rural	Districts with more than 37,000 people or more than 26 per cent of their population in rural settlements and larger market towns.
Rural-50	Districts with at least 50 per cent but less than 80 per cent of their population in rural settlements and larger market towns.
Rural-80	Districts with at least 80 per cent of their population in rural settlements and larger market towns.

Source: Adapted from www.defra.gov.uk, 2008.

'measurement blocks' consisting of about 50 houses or so and which are then classified by both their morphology – or settlement type and their context – or density/sparsity. However, given that more generally a significant amount of other social and economic quantitative information is only available at local authority level this has meant that the older urban/rural local authority classification has not been completely abandoned for output areas. Instead the ways in which local authority urban/rural classification has also been redeveloped by the RERC. The table above sets out this new six tier urban/rural model which is again based purely on numbers, settlement pattern and headcount.

I have spent some time detailing the quantitative framed efforts to pin down the ways as to how rural spaces may be identified and defined. As I noted above these are important because they are used by the key political and policy organisations involved in rural governance and to inform rural policy making and interventions. As an illustration of the 'joined up' policy network interest in finding ways to quantify the countryside it is worth noting that the RERC's Rural Definition was the outcome of a joint project between the Commission for Rural Communities, Defra, the Office for National Statistics, the Office of the Deputy Prime Minister and the Welsh Assembly. The quantitative approaches to defining rurality are also important because they do evidence the range of settlement and density differences across the countryside and in this way highlight the need to recognise diversity in the ways of conceptualising rural spaces. That said the Rural Definition of countrysides – whether Significant Rural, Rural-50 or Rural-80 – all look to be a long way from the emotional and cultural 'countryside of the mind' and as Ray Pahl cautions, 'there are clear limitations on what can be learnt from the analyses of large scale aggregate data that are most likely to have been commissioned by government departments and quangos […] they are more useful for raising interesting questions to investigate than for providing answers' (2007: 7).

The key point I want to make here is that the quantitative rethinking of rural measurement reflects a similar set of concerns to those that influenced the cultural turn of rural studies – namely the economic and social changes taking place in the English countryside. There is a connection between the redesigning of the measurement tools for defining what counts as a rural area and the repositioning of rural studies away from any easily quantifiable premise towards an engagement with what is culturally signified by the category 'the rural'. What both of these shifts do is demonstrate an increasing recognition of rural spaces as undergoing processes of significant social and economical restructuring and change and becoming explicitly uncertain and turbulent terrains and this recognition has demanded revised ways of thinking about those rural spaces. For example the RERC website explains on its homepage how,

> Today, the population of rural England is growing rapidly and, in many places,
> ageing, whilst employment related to land and water based activities directly,

now constitutes only a small proportion (less than 7 per cent) of jobs in rural areas. Over half the jobs in rural areas are now in service activities such as hotels and restaurants, financial services and public administration. These changes are reflected in policy which has moved from a predominant concern with agriculture to a clearer focus on wider social and economic issues.

These changes are also based in what might be called a more 'connected' countryside. As a consequence of increased car ownership there is now much more interchange between rural and urban areas and within rural areas for work, shopping and leisure purposes than even ten years ago and the social and economic 'profiles' of rural localities are now, in most respects, very similar to those of urban England. At the same time, however, many people – the young and the elderly in particular – find it difficult to get access to various services as and when they require them. (www.rerc.ac.uk. Accessed 29 November 2008)

While the debate that took place between Philo, Murdoch and Pratt and Cloke in the *Journal of Rural Studies* in the early 1990s may be more conceptually and radically framed it has also been driven by a concern with the same issues and processes. It is important not see the cultural turn in rural studies as 'ivory tower' navel gazing. It has been driven by and is reflective of the same series of relational changes in the countryside that the RERC notes – a rural economy based less and less on agricultural production and an emergence of a what has been described as a post-productivist countryside (Halfacree, 2007) and a less distinct rural and urban binary – as well as a recognition of issues such as gender, sexuality and poverty (Little, 1997; Hughes, 1997; Cloke, 1995; Valentine, 1997); an increasing commodification of the countryside by tourist and heritage industries; significant middle class urban to rural migration (Halfacree, 1997), and, in the 1980s and 1990s, the high profile insertions of problematised, 'non-rural' figures in rural spaces, notably, for example, New Age Travellers, the Free Party Movement (Sibley, 1995; Cresswell, 1996; Hetherington, 2000), and the beginnings of demands to recognise that there are particular figures who are *assumed* to be rural absence and are *problematised* when they are a rural presence i.e. black and minority ethnic populations (Agyeman, 1989; Agyeman and Spooner, 1997).

These shifts in analytic focus and the opportunities that they have afforded in re-thinking rurality have given rise to such questions as 'what is the rural; what types of representational labour does it do and for whom, and who constitutes rural populations?' Questions such as these emerged as central not only on academic, but also populist and political agendas. This is not to say that such questions had been previously absent – they had not. The Right to Roam protest movements of the 1920s and 1930s, the 19th-century Enclosure Movement, the 18th- and 19th-century Highland Clearances and even the Diggers movement in the 17th century all testify to the longevity of the turbulence of rural spaces and the struggles as to who could or should legitimately be 'in' and part of them. Rather it is to note that since the early 1990s, as the influence of post-modern approaches and the cultural turn in geography, and the social sciences more broadly, took hold, it became a moment for retheorising the category 'the English countryside' and, the notion of rural spaces more broadly.

In particular it was the dominant discourses of the English countryside and the ways in which these obscured the heterogeneity of rural populations and rural experiences and performed some key cultural labour in terms of national identity that became problematised in the new research approaches to understanding rurality. This was a metanarrative in which rural spaces were imagined and represented as picturesque, unchanging sites of social order and deference, of community sameness and familiarity and part of this was a representation of the countryside as a 'white space'. In this way the English countryside was collapsed into a discursive tool of social reassurance. It is the antithesis of the unruly city with its plethora of problems, conflicts and tensions and its multiculture. Within the rural reassurance discourse it was of course necessary to marginalize, invisiblise and subordinate those populations and issues that did not sustain it. In this way dissident and alternative rural dwellers and a range of social problems from poverty, homelessness, racism, unemployment, drug abuse, isolation, inadequate social welfare resources were unaccounted for in notions of what the rural was. Such populations and social problems were effectively erased, marginalised and/ or neglected in academic, populist and governmental approaches to the rural and the countryside.

Rural studies scholars' focus on this hidden-ness and subjugated figures represented a conceptual and methodological embrace of conversations taking place across the social sciences. In particular the concept of 'otherness' has been used as an explanatory tool for making sense of some of contestations over rural identity and its cultural meanings. In uncovering the more concealed aspects of rurality and the countryside, rural studies scholars were arguing for the recognition of an English countryside which was made up of social differences, divisions and exclusions and they were making an argument for the recognition of the ways in which some populations were positioned as apart from, a danger to and other than 'mainstream' rural figures. Developed out of psychoanalysis and the work of Jacques Lacan, post colonial theorists such as Edward Said (1978), Gayatri Spivak (1985) and Homi Bhabha (1990, 1994) have mobilised the concepts of *others* (those threatening, outcast subjects defined in relation to the centre/the Empire/the West) and the dialectical but *ambivalent* process of *othering* (the discursive and material ways in which othered subjects become defined by and simultaneously define the centre or dominant identity) to analyse colonial and post colonial racisms and the patterns and experiences of racialised difference, subordination and exclusion. This ambivalence is important because, as Bhabha argues, it reflects the attraction and repulsion dynamic of the coloniser and colonised relation and shifts it from being one of a straightforward dominant-complaint to a more unsettled power relation. The constant need for the other to remind the centre of what it is and, by extension, is not, means that 'the self-identity of the colonising subject, indeed the identity of imperial culture, is inextricable from the alterity [or apartness] of colonized others' (Ashcroft et al. 1998: 12).

How do such arguments map onto debates about rural identity? It is possible to identify notions of others and processes of othering in the debates about rural identity. Marginalised, subaltern, silenced, undesirable rural figures such as gypsies, travellers, tinkers, tramps are obvious examples and ones which are quite explicitly imbued with senses of fear, fascination and exotica but also those leading alternative lifestyles, the poor, migrant agricultural workers can be understood as being rural others. The social and cultural construction of problem rural populations and 'difficult' and unruly urban–rural figures who do not belong can be understood as part of a process of othering which simultaneously marks out what/who is defined as rurally desirable and conventional and what/who is not. Filtering concerns about rural identity through notions of otherness meant that rural studies was able to avoid a simplistic focus on hidden rurals and invisabilised or problematised rural presences through a relational scrutiny of hegemonic narratives of rural spaces and the 'mainstream' identities of those that inhabited them. In short, the influence of post-colonial and post-modern approaches within rural studies has allowed these to engage and examine the complex interplay of power, politics and representations of social relations and countryside spaces.

This turn was variously captured in a number of edited collections, articles and monographs published in Britain since the mid 1990s which all addressed a range of neglected and marginalised rural identities and the cultural and social meanings attached to the category rural. These edited collections (Cloke and Little, 1997; Milbourne, 1997; Chakraborti and Garland, 2004; Neal and Agyeman, 2006) included chapters on radical environmental protestors; women and gendered experiences of the rural; lesbian communes; children and young people; black and minority ethnic rural residents, workers and visitors; race and ethnicity; migrant agricultural workers, rural poverty and gentrification. Ethnographic research explored New Age Travellers' identities, lifestyles, rural attachments and their (often violently) contested and problematised presence in the English countryside. The theoretical deliberations emphasised the divergent, interdisciplinary routes through which much more *liminal* rural geographies could be conceived.

Deliberations on the Rural: A Metaphor of Nation and a Site of Exclusion

In the post-modern de-coupling of the concept of rurality from the conventional measures and markers of what the countryside is and does, the central theorisation was the ways in which socially and culturally constructed notions of rurality created the rural as a purified and sanctified space requiring (governmental) protection from perceived threats. It is arguments about geographies of purification and exclusion which resonate with a number of the contestations over claims to be in rural spaces. While more recent examples of such contestations in the UK context have been young people and the Free Party movement, New Age Travellers, rurally based asylum seeker centres and migrant agricultural labour these problematised presences are imprinted with the ghosts of earlier struggles perhaps most notably evidenced in urban working class claims to the countryside and the right to roam movement in England in the 1920s and 1930s. It is worth spending a moment detailing the right to roam protests mainly because they historicise the struggles over entitlement and access to rural spaces and evidence the contentions over rural identities and belonging but also because their resolution was an (albeit limited) victory for the rural access movement but also worked was a reinforcement of the relationship between Englishness and rural spaces.

Between the two World Wars there was a vibrant and popular movement that demanded access to the countryside for leisure pursuits, especially for the growing activity of rambling, for the urban-based, working classes. As access to rural areas was regularly and often forcibly denied by landowners despite ancient rights of way and footpaths the right to roam became increasingly politicised as ramblers used the tactic of mass trespass to protest. The first and best known of these mass trespasses was on Kinder Scout in the Derbyshire Peak District during the 1920s and 1930s. Wendy Darby (2000: 128) makes the important point that the Peak District's location in Northern England, with its 'extensive stretches of heather moorland' surrounded by large industrial towns and cities such as Manchester, Sheffield and Derby, helps explain it as a site of intense political activity and bitter conflict. The protests were organised by urban-based ramblers clubs which were often socialist and communist in their political sympathies. While the trespasses were held throughout the interwar years they gathered in momentum and intensity. For example in 1928, 3,000 people took part in 'raids' on Kinder Scout and in April 1932, in what Darby reminds us is still called 'The Mass Trespass', 400 trespassing ramblers were confronted by gamekeepers armed with sticks and clubs and reinforced by police both mounted and with dogs. Six trespass leaders were arrested and charged and five were eventually jailed. Accusations of anti-Semitism (a number of the protestors were Jewish) on the one hand and accusations of communist plots, featured in the trail that received widespread newspaper coverage and meant that issues of access to rural spaces took up a high profile place on the national political agenda (ibid.). This profile was, despite the continued entrenchment of the landowning elites to the notion of rural access and to the trespasses, to play a partial role in the eventual legislative reform and the creation of national parks in the immediate post war period of 'high' social citizenship in Britain. As Matless, (2003) has suggested there are key connections to be made between the Labour government's establishment of the post 1945 welfare state, concerns about social inclusion and the enrolment of rural spaces into this political programme. In the Dower Report (1945) for example there was a recommendation for the need to establish national parks which would be 'extensive tracts of beautiful and wild countryside which would provide scope for open air recreation' (cited in Askins, 2006: 151). The Dower Report informed the eventual Access to the Countryside Act (1949) which oversaw the designation of ten National Parks in the UK during the 1950s and which included the Peak District, which is now the most used and visited of all the National Parks (Darby, 2000).

The right to roam movement is one key narrative of an older struggle for entitlements to exclusionary rural spaces. There are other, older stories too of course – the enclosure and clearance movements mentioned earlier – but of these the right to roam protests capture the particular sanctification of rural space. The protests and their legislative settlement also demonstrated the place of the rural in narratives of national identity. The intimate relationship between notions of the rural and the popular and political national imaginary can be understood as a particularly English phenomenon. However, rural spaces *do* occupy a central place in other narratives of other nations in Europe, in North America and in other Anglophone countries. However, it is important to note that first, these countryside/nation entanglements are differently constructed when compared to the English situation and second, that the English rural was a colonial 'export' and 'comfort' that was recreated and imposed in the rural spaces of the colonised landscapes in Africa and on the Indian sub-continent. It is not unusual, in a routine drive through the countryside surrounding the South African cities of Durban and Cape Town, to pass mock Tudor rural buildings – most often pubs and country clubs. For me, there was a strange disjuncture in seeing the reproduction of English rural geographies and architecture outside of rural England. One example of such a disjuncture occurred when I was in South Africa and on a 'political tour' which included a visit to the site where Nelson Mandela was arrested in 1966. Mandela was at that time in hiding and was living in ANC safe houses and travelling in the rural areas outside of Durban and the place of his arrest is in the remote countryside a few hours from Durban. The actual site is now marked by a plaque but in looking for this our guide and the driver got completely lost. Eventually we stopped at a country club to ask directions. The architecture of club house was closely modelled on the black and white timbered, 1930s buildings that are so reminiscent of rural (and suburban) England. As we listened to the directions being given – we were actually not as lost as we had thought – it was impossible not to notice the large sign announcing that the country club was happy to serve guests, as well as members, Devonshire cream teas. Similar colonial exports of 'the English rural' have been noted in Australia and India too and I return to the question of a more global context in terms of how and in what ways rural spaces relate to national imaginaries below (and in Chapter 7).

I rather deliberately selected this vignette from South Africa with all its explicit connections to 'extreme race politics' as it has been perhaps been the relationship between rurality, race and ethnicity that has driven much of the scrutiny of the representational work that the English countryside does assembling the dominant (if anodyne) markers of Englishness. However, in many ways this scrutiny has had to contend with processes in which the English countryside works as a *de-racialised* landscape. The term de-racialised is used here to refer to the duality by which race is denied as being a key referent in a discourse that is very much about race. In dominant rural imaginaries and rural spaces the notion of race is deemed irrelevant as the spaces have been subject to a hyper whitening process as the concept of race and the presence of black and other minority ethnic figures and populations are written out assumed as an absence, as distant or as uninterested. The attempt to extract or write out race from popular concepts of rurality reveals the extent to which whiteness is able to deny and position itself as a (none) category outside of race thinking and identification. What writing out of race also does is actively shape a national narrative in which the English countryside is valorised as an inert, culturally homogenous, 'forever England' place that is able to work as a symbolic space of whiteness.

What are the material and everyday outcomes of this? As I have argued elsewhere (see Neal, 2002) some of the rural otherness and ethnicity debate has also been concerned with the extent to which black and minority ethnic rural residents and rural visitors experience racism, harassment, violence and racialised marginalisation (Garland and Chakraborti, 2007) and the extent to which rural spaces are underused and perceived as not easily accessible or welcoming to black and minority ethnic populations (Agyeman and Spooner, 1997) although as Askins (2006: 155) warns it is important not to 'over race' this reticence as black and minority perceptions of the countryside are likely to be shaped by a range of factors. The de-racialised rural discourse does performs a number of concerning tasks: it denies and makes invisible the small, scattered but significant and increasing numbers of black and minority ethnic residents, workers and visitors in rural areas; it severely limits the multicultural sensibility of rural policy makers, service deliverers and those responsible for rural well-being; it sweeps under the historical carpet the longevity and proximity of the colonial-countryside relation. For example the stately homes beloved of organisations such as the National Trust and English Heritage were built with colonial acquired wealth and their interiors are often influenced by and designed to reflect a 'colonial aesthetic'. The huge grounds of these country houses are planted with trees, flowers and shrubs brought from colonised countries. As Scruton notes, 'the ambition of the English gentleman was not to spend his money in London, still less to squander it in the colonies where so much of it was made. It was to bring money home to his country retreat, and there embellish the house, the landscape and the gardens (2000: 38). And as I have noted elsewhere (Neal, 2002) the names of some rural villages and public houses and domestic houses testify to a colonial familiarity. For example although now renamed, my next door neighbours' rather grand 18th-century house in the North Norfolk village where I lived for a time was originally called Mysore House. What the de-racialisation of rural spaces has been most effective at doing is in producing a potent and reiterative narrative in which a purified spatialisation of ethnicity and multiculture occurs – ethnicity and multiculture 'belong to' and 'are of' urban environments and do not 'belong to' and are 'not of' rural environments. While there are of course constant challenges as well as quantitative (2001 Census data for example) and qualitative evidence (Tyler, 2006 for example) which counter and disrupt this narrative it retains a populist and political tenacity in the UK.

Unstable Rurality: The Unfinished Process of Securing the Nation

There is clearly, from a policy perspective among others, a need to rethink the de-racialised rural discourse for two reasons. First, it is a discourse which denies and conceals the increase in rural multiculture which impacts on the everyday experiences of living, working or visiting rural areas. There is now a relatively significant body or research and literature which documents and examines these and makes recommendations for those organisations, policy makers and service deliverers with responsibility for rural well-being to recognise and respond to the realities of multicultural populations living in areas outside of those to which they are assumed to be resident in (see for example Jay, 1992; Derbyshire, 1994; Dahlech, 1999; Neal, 2002; Connolly, 2006; Williams, 2007; Garland and Chakraborti, 2007).

Second, the whitening of rural spaces has not been about whiteness *per se*. The whiteness that has been imagined in rural areas is particularly grained and hierarchically constructed as to its social and political desirability. As the discussions above show whiteness has never simply equated to belonging in racialised narratives. In rural spaces there have been problematised, outcast, white presences in both historical and contemporary countryside environments and these have been variously met with local and national hostility culminating in restrictive legislation.

Alongside a privileging of cultural sameness, the English rural discourse has, in particular, been about social order. The countryside idyll and 'village England' represent a highly regulated, socially deferential space. It reflects a particular form of hierarchy and control perhaps most obviously seen in the squirearchy local social system and it reflects a bigger scale political system: the country house, land ownership and the country seat provided the basis of the traditionalist political organisation of England. While Woods (2005: 46) details the shifts in balances of political power away from these older landowning models he maintains that 'the local power structure of most rural areas at the start of the 21st century is still essentially elitist.' Despite the various political changes that have taken place in the governance of rural populations over the 20th and 21st centuries, there is still a strong association between rural spaces and the notion of social order and deferentially inflected social stability. It is this that gets regularly and evocatively called on in times of political crisis and anxiety both historically and contemporarily as much of this book argues.

During World War I it was a ruralist version of England and particularly southern England that was emphasised, mobilised and idealised as 'home'. Alun Howkins suggests that this idyllisation of the south of England worked as a powerful antithesis to the geography and war horrors of Flanders. The ways in which WW1 worked with and produced a rural idyll of the English nation was multidimensional. It threaded through the writing of war poets like Siegfried Sassoon, Edward Thomas and Edmund Blunden of course but it was there in the imaginings and dreamings of fields and lanes and cottages that ordinary soldiers wrote of in their letters and correspondence home and, as a measure of the effectiveness of ruralism it can be read into the increase, in the post-World War I period, of ex-soldiers buying plot land and shanty building in the countryside (Howkins, 1986: 80–81). In World War II it was again the Southern counties of England that provided the rich ruralist propaganda of the home/nation that was being defended. The Imperial War Museum in London has some magnificent examples of such posters showing 'classic' views across the English South Downs with little cottages and farms nestled in the curves of the hills. It was exactly these images that were selected to instill fortitude in the population and act as visual reminder of the nation. The mobilisation of a ruralist versions of nation are not confined to the extreme political moments of war. As Murdoch and Pratt (1997: 56) put it 'the rural is easily portrayed as a 'civilised retreat [...] a zone where Sameness (British or English middle class whiteness and heterosexuality) is reasserted in the wake of profound post-colonial anxiety'. It is possible to see some of this anxiety at work in the reflections of the political and populist right. Conservative politicians in particular have drawn on such images, from Home Secretary William Whitelaw recounting the rural view from his garden as urban unrest spread across inner city areas of Britain to former Prime Minister John Major suggesting that a gentle ruralism would continue to define a Britain of the future (see Chapter 4). Conversely, the more recent attempts to define the UK through different and urban narratives such as the cosmopolitan and multiculturally inflected story of 'Cool Britannia' – packaged as a young, urban, art, music and style renaissance – was troubled and largely unsuccessful. More successful was the campaign for the 2012 Olympics in which London was represented and explicitly celebrated for its multiculturalism and ethnic diversity – it was 'the whole world within one city'. However this was a London story rather than a new story of England. Indeed throughout the late 1990s and the early 2000s the New Labour government, with its metropolitan associations, had a particularly turbulent relationship with the countryside (see Woods, 2005 for example).

While there was the legislation on reforming and developing open access to the countryside (Countryside and Rights of Way Act, 2000) most obvious battleground New Labour's contested engagement with the politics of the rural were of course played out in the controversial fox hunting ban legislation and the high profile emergence of the politically traditionalist and conservative Countryside Alliance (Woods, 2005: 101–130). Not only did the Countryside Alliance show itself to be highly politically organised – there were three large scale national marches held in central London for example – but it was able to present the Alliance as the *authentic* voice of the countryside and of rural values. The Countryside Alliance successfully managed to allude to, borrow and adapt from the political language and images associated with previous and radical social justice campaigns and then apply these to a stark rural–urban oppositional binary (see Neal and Agyeman, 2006). In particular, the Alliance focused its arguments with the government around the theme of freedom and national identity – the fox hunting ban provided the context for the Alliance to make effective links between over regulation, notions of a national rural culture and everyday rural practices and freedom and distil this into an argument of rural populations constituting a minority cultural group (ibid.: 107–108). While the close connections between ideas of rural spaces and ideas of liberty and an absence of regulation is taken up in Chapter 6 it is important to note that the Countryside Alliance's mobilisation of freedom – seen for example in very deliberately named Liberty and Livelihood demonstration – with a national

Figure 2.1   A 'Real' Countryside Alliance sticker – North Norfolk, September 2005

(*Note*: The Real CA is a radical splinter group of the original Countryside Alliance and responsible for the 'high spectacle' political statements on landscapes such as placing a Love Hunting banner on the Angel of the North statue. (Woods, 2005: 128))

identity being endangered by a metropolitan elite was of course that old sleight of hand in which the rural becomes a container for, and symbol of a particular version of Englishness albeit one injected with a the new twist of the conservative use of radical social justice politics. The image of the green Union Jack with the phrase FREE COUNTRY at the centre – which could be regularly seen stuck on road signs and village signs in rural areas in the early 2000s – works effectively in its visual representation of this folding in of the rural–the nation/countryside–national values theme.

This particular and necessarily narrow imagining of the rural has held a long appeal for the political right – not only for those with conservative tendencies but also for those on the extreme right in Britain. The latter have, with a passing nod to the rurally focused racialised terror activities of the Ku Klux Klan in the United States (Iganski and Levin, 2004), increasingly been concerned with attempting to organise around and disseminate via their newsletter 'Land and People', a notion of rural Britain as the last outpost of an imagined Englishness and the need for it to be 'defended' as such. The British National Party has tapped into those explicitly raced elements of urban to rural migrants that some of the early research on racism in rural areas documented. For example Eric Jay describes some of his participants as openly describing themselves as 'refugees from multiracialism' (1992: 22). Similarly in her work in Norfolk Helen Derbyshire was told by one policy maker that 'some people come to Norfolk for "quality of life" and the white complexion of the area has something to do with that quality of life' (1994: 21). The focus on a rural agenda has delivered the British National Party some political successes notably winning councillor seats in Worsthorne a rural village in Northern England in local elections in the early 2000s (ibid.; Neal and Agyeman, 2006). While the far right interest in rural spaces and the racist reading of them as 'white spatial refuge' does have potential to disrupt the de-racing of English rural spaces, far right activities do remain relatively marginal. This idea of race being an uncommented on absence in English rural spaces is a contrast to other national settings. In the United States for example the history of the Deep South and the history of Native American Indians mean that rural landscapes are deeply entangled with African-American culture, racial violence, segregation and racial inequality. In Australia too the rural base of Australian Aboriginal settlement, culture and struggles fundamentally recasts the rural others debates. In postcolonial Zimbabwe and Kenya and post apartheid South Africa the high profile contestations over white owned farms and land rights again prohibits the sanitisation and purification of rural spaces.

Much of the rural identity and rural otherness debates have been situated within a very British and often, very English, context. In many ways this 'parochialness' reflects the cultural, social and political cornerstone that the concept of rurality has taken up in the dominant narratives and formations of national identity. The sanctification and associated regulation of rural spaces have been about the cultural representations and constructions of Englishness and, at various historical and contemporary moments, at the heart of political and policy processes. For example, as I noted above, until the early 20th century the country house was integral to class and political systems in Britain. In policy terms in Britain the imagined and material distinction between country and city has been firmly maintained with the help of the Green Belt planning regulations which aimed to protect the countryside and stop the urban and suburban sprawl. At a moment of affluent counter urbanisation, rural repopulation and current debates as to the future of the Green Belt policy the contestations over rural space and how it is used and by whom is as intense as ever. As Michael Bell notes, in the UK from English literature to the regulation of land planning there is a fetishisation of rural spaces 'from the perspective of the rest of the Anglophone world, the United Kingdom has a stunningly complex and restrictive array of laws which seek to preserve the country's rural character. Although comparable changes have affected the United States and Canada and Australia, these countries have not produced comparable literatures or planning efforts surrounding the edge of pastoral nature' (1994: 10).

Nevertheless the specificity of the British case does *not* mean that rural spaces do not shape and influence other nations' narratives and signifiers of national identity – other European countries, and as Bell (1994) observes Australia, Canada and the US for example – all incorporate and mobilise rural spaces as representational markers and signifiers of nation. Nor is this to suggest that such narratives do not contain rural folk devils and rural others. The hostility and animosity towards Gypsies in Eastern Europe and Travellers in the Irish Republic evidence (Connolly, 2006). Rather, it is to suggest that those narratives have not constructed sanctified, purified and regulated rural spaces to the same *totalising* extent. Rural poverty and issues of race (the early European migrant settlers, the 'forty acres and a mule' end of slavery settlement; the racial segregation and violence of the Deep South, the Dust Bowl migrants, the coal mining communities in the Appalachian Mountains and so forth) have not been erased from the US national story – indeed to some extent – albeit in a romanticised and/or historicised form, it is integral to it. In a different example which nevertheless demonstrates the same point researchers have argued that the reason that the New Age Traveller controversy has died down in the context of the British countryside is because many New Age Travellers have moved to mainland European rural spaces. Although these are not without trespass laws, policing and regulation, New Age Travellers have not been viewed with the same intense anxiety and so are not perceived as requiring legislation and subject to draconian policing (Hetherington, 2000). However, as New Age Travellers have diminished as cultural and social threat within English countrysides than the vacated space has been taken up with the emergence of often crudely articulated anxieties about asylum seekers and migrant agricultural workers in rural and semi-rural environments. The New Labour governments feted and then abandoned plans (vociferously opposed by local residents) to convert disused airbases in parts of rural Nottinghamshire and Worcestershire in 2002 are one of the most obvious examples of this. As Les Back (2007) notes the issues of race have escaped from their traditional containment of the inner city as more recent forms of contested migrations – for example migrant workers, asylum seekers and refugees – have become associated with smaller cities and towns and particularly seaside towns. In a reflection of the multi-ethnicity of England on the one hand and of the global movement of peoples on the other what is increasingly apparent is the impossibility of separating the English countryside from these and suggesting that rural spaces are not as much part of these processes as urban spaces. More than anything though what these contestations and mobilisations demonstrate is the politically unsettled character of rural spaces.

Conclusion

This chapter has been suggested that the concept of otherness usefully transfers to rural spaces – not only because of the relationship between rural spaces and representations of nation and because these require 'outcast' populations to define and add content or meanings to them, but also because rural spaces are themselves imprinted with the histories of colonialism. However, what I want to suggest is that despite the consolidation of a growing body of literature that incorporates notions of otherness and advances conceptions of rurality and the ways in which rural spaces are enrolled into national narratives with exclusionary material outcomes, this has had only a limited and uneven impact on rural policy development and policy delivery in the English countryside. There are social and economic related politics and conflicts of the rural that are conducted in the mainstream and very public arenas – who could ignore the hunting debate, controversies about the location of wind farms, housing development plans, the closure of rural post offices, fears about GM crops and Avian bird flu as well as worries about the impact of house prices and high levels of second home ownership? But in populist and political terms the English countryside still manages to remain entrenched in its seductive offerings of secure spaces – in need of protection from the effects of larger social changes and under contestant threat and endangered perhaps – but nevertheless, with a remarkable tenacity, rural spaces seem adept at being able to remain successfully operating as a complex point of assemblage in which private and public desire and anxiety and affection converge. In other words English rural spaces continue to be able to work as and present as spatialised reassurances of social order and certainty. They not only continue to do so – and this is a key trouble of this book – but they increasingly take up this role in the face of rising ontological insecurities and uncertainties about national identity. This is the point made by Vron Ware when she notes that 'Britain is an old country, wherever you decide to date its origins. It has been around long enough to have survived layers of identity crises, regardless of who or what provoked them. But the old stories that kept it going no longer do the trick' (2007: 2). It is within the vacuum of identification then rural spaces have become a particular focus of contestation and argument. In no small part it is because rural spaces appear to present both an 'ancient world' but also a natural world and it is this ability to draw on the social and the non-human that gives it its intensity and its flexibility in terms of it appeal and its ability to offer comfort and security. The rural, as a container of ethnic identification, familiarity and orderliness, works with and through the social and with, and through, nature. In the concept of the rural the social and nature continually leak into, and borrow from, each other. We can see this exact process at work for example in novelist Joanna Trollope's comments in the *Sunday Telegraph* on the Countryside Alliance's high profile Liberty and Livelihood march through central London:

> There is something singular about the relationship between the English and their countryside...a robust instinct for living in practical harmony with nature (resulting in that much admired social unit, the English village), and an almost pantheistic appreciation of landscape...*the English continue to feel a determined union with the countryside*. It is a sense of belonging and finding salvation there, in a community – preferably consisting of a church, pub, farms, cottages, a small school and a Big House. We have, we English, a national village cult: we cherish the myth out there, among fields and woods, there still survives a timeless natural innocence and lack of corruption. (1998: 1 cited in Woods, 2005: 116. Emphasis added)

I have quoted Trollope at length here because of her of presentation of English ethnicity as profoundly entangled with and collapsible into the countryside (i.e. nature) and with community (i.e. the social). While the focus of rural otherness debates and worries about processes of rural exclusion have been primarily on social relations there has been a neglect of the ways in which nature is incorporated and actively shapes those social relations. Trollope is specific in her definitions of what a rural community looks like. Her outline of the architecture and the type of social institutions that constitutes a rural community reflect the extent to which the notion of rural community acts as a condensation symbol (Edelman, 1977). In particular it acts as a condensation symbol of social stability and order. This social order is organically framed and located – it emerges from and is embedded in fields and woods – and it carries with it an innate political 'goodness' or 'wholesomeness'.

It is exactly this model of a rural community that has been of concern within sociology more broadly and within the critical rethinking of the rural studies approach. However these critical concerns with these closed, 'golden age' conceptualisations of rural spaces and the communities that exist within them have underestimated the extent to which the notion of the rural village community is cherished both within the rural imaginary and wider populist thinking. It is these key aspects of community – the relationship of the concept to the rural; the durability and the emotional appeal of the concept and its naturalisation within pastoral landscapes that is the focus of the next chapter.

Chapter 3
Mapping Rurality:
Community and Countrysides

Introduction

Community is, as I have argued earlier, a troubled but durable social science concept. Part of its troubles – and its tenacity – is the concept's ability to reach out far beyond the academic world and connect with the ways in which people chose to make sense of their and others social relations. While it works across time and space (see Mooney and Neal, 2009 for example) more than anything community works as a potent container of and symbol for the ways in which rural social relations are organised. This is what I suggested is captured in Joanne Trollope's comments cited in the previous chapter – community summons up and becomes interchangeable with the idea of village, the location of the village, the institutions of the village, the members of the village and the processes and rhythms of village life. As Graham Day argues 'as places in which agricultural work is done, villages tend to be looked upon as long established, slow growing, close to nature, and in harmony with their environment, surely the most "organic" of human contexts... the village type of social setting epitomises the social wholeness many expect from community' (2006: 40).

What this chapter sets out to examine is the way in which this community-rural relationship works with such proximity in both social science research and deliberations and in everyday rural contexts. The chapter begins by acknowledging the assumptions, ambiguities and anxieties that are associated with the concept of community before tracing the extent to which it has shaped social research agendas. The final sections of the chapter will argue that the contemporary re-engagement with community and its populist ascendancy reflect the concept's uncanny ability to work as a post-modern longing for pre-modern forms of social relations. In the late modernity's era of individualism, risk perception and uncertainty (see Cochrane and Talbot, 2008) community appears to offer security and stability not least because at its heart community is a process of social encounters and interactions which has to include some and simultaneously exclude others.

The Trouble with Community

It has become something of a sociological 'given' that using the concept of community is asking for trouble (I return to this issue in Chapter 5). Writing in 1971 (p.13) Howard Newby reminds us that as early as 1966 (p.148) Ruth Glass had condemned community studies as 'the poor sociologist's substitute for the novel'. For Glass the descriptive nature of community research and its absence of quantitative data meant that community studies could be taken as no more than a non-comparative set of time and place specific social stories. The sociological disillusionment with community as an object of inquiry was further hastened by sociology's move, in the 1970s, away from geography and towards an embracing of formations of identity and imagination. Community became revisited as a non-spatially based concept and from this as a site in which co-constituting processes of inclusion and exclusion occurred, were reproduced and were reinforced. In other words the cosy, organic community described by Trollope in the Chapter 2 concealed the extent to which communities operated as boundaries and zones in which people were kept out and zones in which the behaviour of those that were included was heavily regulated.

While I return to these arguments in more detail below and in Chapter 5 what I want to suggest here is that although social science may be cautious about community and its ability, as a concept, to analyse social relationships this has not diminished its dominance within social science nor has it diminished its dominance in wider social and everyday settings. I have argued elsewhere (Mooney and Neal, 2009) that community carries an intense attraction for politicians, policy makers but it also has a 'folk' appeal. On this basis it is crucial for social science to retain a concern with community and to be engaged by what it appears to be able to offer and gives it its populism. In other words community is impossible to ignore (even though the contentions as to how it gets used as an analytical tool for understanding contemporary social relations remain). This folk appeal emerged repeatedly within the project and I want to think through the trouble with community by looking at an extended extract from one of the project's focus group interviews.

The notion that the countryside was synonymous with socially caring rural communities dominated the participants' conversations within the interviews. This does not mean that the conversations were identical – for some rural communities were under threat from a variety of sources, for others rural communities were alive and flourishing but certainly the conversation that is presented below captures a very common experience that was expressed in the focus group interviews:

> Ava: I organise the British Legion Poppy round and my round takes me so long because I know the people so well. It takes a long time because people say 'alright well come along and have a cup of tea'. [Lots of laughter] It takes a long time but you don't mind, it's nice.

Audrey: I used to find that when collecting the Children Society boxes. It was a real social event. [Lots of yeses]

Irene: It's because everybody knows everybody. (Haverfield WI, North Devon)

There will be more conversations very similar to those being made by Ava, Audrey and Irene throughout the book. But my point here is that there was a reiterated emphasis that was put on the Gemeinschaft *social* village by participants across the three case study areas and across the different types of focus groups. In other words despite the gendered and age profile differences of the Women's Institute and Young Farmers participants there was a continually articulated and shared engagement with a notion of community.

While this commitment to community carried anxieties with it – was it under threat from outsiders, urban migrants, the closure of social resources, agricultural changes and so forth – any explicit discussions of community tensions and social divisions were almost non-existent. Challenges made within the focus group interviews to *Gemeinschaft* narratives tended to be limited and very much framed within the bounds of what the rest of the group agreed with. More diverse or competing narratives were then more difficult to elicit and access. This difficulty is best captured in the Appleby WI discussion when Ruth, who had lived in the village since 1987, alludes to her senses of isolation and social divisions within the village:

Ruth: I mean I found that the only way that I was meeting people was through the WI or through the pub or things like that. But I think that a lot of people who've got dogs or children at school do meet the villagers but…I find it quite a classy type of village. There's a lot of class distinctions in the village. I don't know if you think that? [This question is to the rest of the group]

Others: Never noticed it.

No.

No.

But you're in the middle/

Ruth: We're right in the middle of two different classes of people.

Olive: I suppose you are yes.

Others: Yes, yes.

Ruth: Yes.

Researcher: When you say in the middle do you mean physically?

Ruth: Our house is physically in the middle if people who are yeah well off and/

Sylivia: Yes.

Ruth: And who actually work on the farm, they used to be farm labourers.

Laura: That's right, yes.

Ruth: And it's, it's still there…as far as the class society, which I know people hate that word but I still think its around, would you say fifty–fifty?

Jan: I wouldn't have thought that much now…There is no squire here now is there?

Sylivia: No.

Jan: And to me it's classless but that's just the way I am. (Page 4 of transcript)

It is possible to see from this exchange that Ruth offers her observations about class to the group to verify. However her claim is particularised by the other group members and attributed not to the village but to Ruth's two neighbours. When Ruth tries again to assert a half-and-half division in the village this is rejected by Jan. Reading the transcript of this discussion it is possible to see how Ruth's comments on social difference in the village continue to linger over the group's conversation. For example, later in the discussion it is returned to:

Pip: …yes there's a huge mixture and mostly we get on fine but there's always an odd one…

Jan: Ruth was saying about the different classes but I do find they mix.

[Lots of voices]

Ann: I think Ruth agreed with that.

Pip: Most of us mix. (Page 11 of transcript)

Again the idea that there are divisions within the village are raised but it is the harmonious 'mixing' community that is quickly re-asserted. While support for Ruth is voiced within the group it is expressed in terms of Ruth having conceded to the argument on mixing. Much further into the discussion Ruth's comments on isolation and division is again reintroduced by Olive, a long established resident of the village.

Olive: I find it more sort of friendly than say Ruth does, she feels more of a split, I never did.

Ruth: Well I probably said that wrongly/

Olive: No, no (Ruth is trying to carry on speaking and justify/explain what she meant) and I think it depends on your attitude… (Page 26 of transcript)

Ruth's introduction of the issues of class and loneliness works like a whisper of another story albeit one that is pushed to the margins of this focus group's conversation. However this is not completely successful as it does continue to appear and disappear in their discussions (I have provided the transcript page numbers to help convey a sense its presence within the group's overall discussion). The excerpt above marks the final reference to Ruth's comment. In saying that she 'said it wrongly' Ruth distances herself from the idea of a divided village community.

It is not clear what Ruth's experiences of the focus group interview have been. It may have been an uncomfortable experience in that she alone offered a more critical version of life in their village. It is interesting that, towards the end of the group's conversation, it is Ruth who suddenly questions the researcher's questions. In doing so she opens up the legitimacy of the researcher's presence in the group. It emerges after a long discussion about the local landscape and what it is that makes them feel at home in it:

> Ruth [to the researcher]: Why are you so interested in what we like? [The project had been explained to participants and the group had all signed a consent form on which the aims of the project were listed]
>
> Researcher: Because we're, one of the things we're interested in is about people's feeling about the landscape and what that has to do with their feeling about who they are…
>
> Penny: It seems to be quite a theme with us.
>
> [Lots of people saying yes]
>
> Jan: We like where we live. (Page 41 of transcript. Appleby WI, Hertfordshire)

It is certainly possible to read a (re)positioning here of the researcher as an outsider. The raising of the strangeness of the researcher's presence/questions works as a reminder to the researcher of her status within the group. At the same time as the groups expresses an agreement that there is a relationship between where they live and how they identify themselves there is a certain inclusive defiance in Jan's, 'We like where we live' comment which is made in almost the very last moments of the interview.

I have quoted at length from the Appleby conversation because it captures a cluster of the concerns that accompany the use of community and with which this chapter engages:

- The dominance of the 'complete' community discourse
- The seductions of community
- Researching rural communities

It is to these that the chapter now turns.

Studies of Rural Community

I have argued in my analysis of the Appleby conversation that there was a shared reticence by those participating in the focus group interview to engage in discussions (revelations?) about conflict and tension within the village. While this reticence can be attributed to a multiple of factors – researchers as outsiders; the collective nature of focus groups; the desire to give a best narrative of place – the reluctance in Appleby to be open about class and the corresponding containing of Ruth's contributions within the group does mirror one of the key troubles of community – the ways in which community works to produce conformity and regulate social practices – this means there is little room for individual dissent and difference. There is an absence of discussion of this aspect of community in some of the early rural community focussed research in the UK.

The work of American anthropologists Arensberg and Kimball (1940) in County Clare, Ireland and Welsh geographer Alwyn Rees (1950) in Montgomeryshire, Wales is largely silent on the notion of divisions and antagonism within social relations in their case study areas. Both of these studies presented the themes of family, kinship and neighbourliness as core to explaining local social systems in rural settlement and arguing that these were cohesive, interdependent and complete or whole social systems. It is this *completeness* that gives the inhabitants of Llanfihangel yng Ngwynfa – the parish that formed the basis of Rees' largely qualitative study – their sense of belonging and social bonds. Rees' study in particular is threaded through by a sense of weakening social ties and imminent change under the influences of 'modern urban society' – 'the little community in Llanfihangel, though accepting current values and becoming part of the contemporary economic system is already in the initial stages of social atomisation…The further one proceeds from the countryside the more narrowly concerned do people become in their own specialised little worlds, the more lacking in social wholeness' (1950: 168). Although Bell and Newby (1971: 140) suggest that Rees overstates his anti-urban position and strays too close into 'community as normative prescription [rather] than empirical description' they go on to argue that Rees 'can be considered the founding father of the British community study – over the next fifteen years the prefaces of most studies acknowledge a debt to him'. Rees' account of Llanfihangel can be read as a contribution to a 'golden age' metanarrative of the rural community story. For example Rees emphasises the mutuality between neighbours and the home as key to the community in Llanfihangel: 'By friendliness towards his neighbours the countryman overcomes the isolation imposed on him by his environment. By welcoming them to his home, by visiting them in their turns, by helping them in their troubles and by co-operating with them in the performance of certain kinds of farm work, he maintains a form of society which dispenses with the functions of a central meeting place at a village or town. From his contacts with his neighbours the individual derives both companionship and assistance' (1950: 91). But his study has value too in terms of its observational descriptions of aspects of social relations in remote rural locations in the 1930s and 1940s. Rees stresses the importance of conviviality and hospitality – community is based around *informal* sociality and the organised in homes; 'home has been the place at which people gathered for a noson lawen (merry evening), for religious devotions and above all for conversation' (ibid.: 100). Rees' Llanfihangel research was influential in later studies of rural populations but also, as Harold Carter (1996) has noted, it should be recognised as marking a recasting of the anthropological gaze away from the exotic other of colonial contexts and onto the familiar social and geographies of 'home'.

However, the tendency that Rees exemplified towards the telling an observational story of an anti-urban cohesive rural community was further developed in the research of William Morgan Williams'– who had been a student of Alwyn Rees – 1956 study of the rural community of Gosforth in the Lake District. Although the Gosforth study focussed on class and social status – Williams used seven categories of class to examine social systems and relations he nevertheless argued that family, kinship and neighbourliness were all highly interactional and able to work across these categories.

According to Williams Gosforth could be understood as a 'close-knit', face to face based, rural community. However, as Bell and Newby point out for Williams, as for Rees, there is a worry that the stability of Gosforth is likely to shift and change as urban and outside influences *negatively* impact on these localities with 'a loss of community feeling because of these developments' (1956: 202). While Bell and Newby are critical of the absence of quantative measures by which to compare these early community studies what is more striking well over half a century on is the extent to which the notion of imminent change to rural populations – particularly from an urban outside – casts a perennial shadow over these studies. It is this that can be heard in some of the interview conversations in my study, as Chapter 7 will explore further, but the following extract from a Hertfordshire based Young Farmers Club is cited here in order to illustrate not simply their sense of loss of a 'whole community' but an unease in articulating this. The members of this focus group are nearly all connected to farming and had lived in Hertfordshire almost all of their lives. For members of this group there was a predominant narrative in which they, and 'their rural heritage', are threatened by the 'old danger' of gypsies on the one hand and a 'newer danger' of wealthy urban incomers on the other. However, at the end of the discussion it is clear that there is some anxiety about appearing as too hostile to outsiders as this extract from the interview shows:

> Dave: What do you think of us then? What do we come across as? As you've been sitting there, from a town? [Laughter in the group]

> Researcher: You're putting me on the spot now! What do I think of you in terms of whether you're country people?

Dave: Yeah. Do you think we're a bunch of whiners?

Researcher: Not at all. Oh no. I don't think you're whiners at all. No it's been very interesting.

Steve: She's just saying that.

Researcher: Do I lie so badly! [Laughing and then serious.] No. Actually what you have said has been very interesting. Really. You've been saying things I wasn't expecting you to say.

Paul: Are your views the same as ours then or not? What we're saying, do you agree with what we're saying?

Researcher: Well I don't know, I don't know because I've always lived in a city or town. I've never even lived in a village so I don't know any of those perspectives. But it's good to hear them… (Waterdon YFC, Herfortshire)

There are clearly anxieties here evidenced by the group's demand to know what the researcher thinks, the harsh self-description as 'whiners' and the need to know how their perspectives are received. While the researcher does seek to respond to this anxiety and reassure the focus group members when she is pushed by Paul to reveal her own thoughts she invokes her distance and stresses her urban, *non-rural* identity as a strategy for avoiding having to openly associate or disassociate herself from the conversation that has taken place. This does not dispel the groups worries though. Their ambivalence about their construction of an insider and outsider boundary can be heard in the conditionality of rural settlement which is expressed by one of the group:

It's not that we're against townspeople. [Lots of 'Nos' from the group.] They are more than welcome to come to the countryside as long as they don't make a mess and respect our way of life and don't want to change it.

While the Rees and Williams studies do engage with the processes of social change within local rural communities they both assert that the interactional wholeness of those communities was their strongest and most dominant feature. Later studies of rural communities in the UK began to engage more fully with the ways in which community in rural areas had to be understood as a stratified concept defined by notions of division, boundaries and outsiders.

Howard Newby's (1977) study of farm labourers in East Anglia was one of the first that marked the beginning of this repositioning of the both method and theoretical focus. In arguing that a class analysis based on land and property ownership was as relevant in rural societies as urban ones Newby that the English peasantry had, since the 19th century, been replaced with a class system and social division between the working class agricultural labourers and the distinctly middle class of farmers, landowners and professionals (clergy/teachers/incomers). While for Newby this meant that conflict had to be viewed as integral to rural social relations he argued that this conflict was to greater and lesser extents contained by the dominance of the authoritarian and deferential narratives of the village community. Newby (1977: 46) argued that community could be seen in the ways in which working class agricultural labourers had,

> a strong sense of shared occupational experience, a distinctive occupational culture, an overlap between work and non-work roles and loyalties, a prevalence of closely knit cliques of friends, workmates, neighbours and relatives and generally a *strong sense of group identity which marked off the village from the others that surrounded it*. This strong sense of attachment to primary groups was partly a function of geographical isolation and a common occupation, but it was also forged out of the economic necessities of living close to poverty which promoted values of mutual aid and neighbourliness. (Emphasis added)

Alongside this version of a local rural community of fate and necessity Newby suggested it was possible to see another narrative of the village community into which both labourer and landowner/farmer could all belong. This narrative is one which focuses on the whole village and its territorial geography and folds social inequality into this. This produces a cohesion and village narrative that exists more as a subjective construct – what Ray Pahl (1979) called the 'village of the mind' (see also Strathern, 1982: 250–1) – rather than an objective, measurable reality. As Newby argues,

> The encouragement of localism enabled identification with the social system to prevail by emphasising a common adherence to territory, a solidarity of place, encompassing both elite and subordinates alike. The traditional landowning class placed an ideological gloss on their monopoly of power within the locality through the concept of 'community'. 'Community' as an ideology became superimposed onto the reality of the village community as a social system so that it becomes very difficult to disentangle the two. (1977: 52)

Recalling the conversation in the Appleby Women's Institute focus group that was cited earlier there is certainly something of the 'village of the mind' that can be seen in the 'closing down' of Ruth and any explicit discussion of division and the assertion of a meta-narrative of local community and of social belonging that can work over and above socio-economic lines of stratification. However Newby's conceptualisation of this meta-narrative as being 'superimposed' sounds overly mechanical and functionalist. Ruth distances herself from her comments and concedes completely to the others in the group and the group is to some extent protective of her – remember for example the contributor who notes that 'I think Ruth agreed with that'. What I would suggest is that the notion of a 'village community' is one that has a meaning which is able to work beyond any concrete everyday realities and it is this imagined community that is made purchase on from both above and below. I shall return to this in later chapters and in my discussion of

Michael Bell's (1994) study of Childerley but it is worth noting that the imagined rural community is one that is able to contain and manage social division and is an imagining that is invested in from below as well as above. Here I am following Marilyn Strathern's (1982) recasting of Newby's community as social construct thesis in her own study of the village of Elmdon in Essex in the 1960s.

While Strathern focussed on notions of kinship and belonging rather than class in the village she, like Newby, found a series of social stratifications. However, Strathern argues that the boundary mechanisms between the social categories of Elmdon society interacted with, rather than were defined by, land and property ownership and did so in a complexly defined hierarchy of social relations. For example Strathern identifies four broad (and class corresponding) social groupings in Elmdon – 'real Elmonders' (born and bred in Elmdon families); 'Elmdoners' (Real Elmdoners which had married in outsider family members before 1914); working class newcomers (post-1914) and middle class commuters and retirees (post-1914). From this Strathern argues that Newby's narrative of 'whole village community' imposed from above by the property classes was not seen in Elmdon as 'Real Elmonders' resisted this and spoke of a divided village while middle class incomers did claim that a village community existed. Yet Strathern does concur with Newby in her acknowledgement that 'the cultural elements out of which their [i.e. real Elmdoners and middle class newcomers] models are constructed are largely shared. There is broad agreement about what it *means* to be a "villager" or "outsider" and most of the inhabitants subscribe to the idea that the village is bounded' (1982: 253. Emphasis in original).

It is worth recalling the Appleby conversation here and the group's assertion of a whole village community as it reflects both a Newby and a Strathern analysis of assertions of villages of belonging *despite* internal divisions. In Elmdon, there may be a diminishing core of 'real villagers' but these are added to by various others who do nevertheless belong to Elmdon. For Strathern the relationship between belonging and the social boundaries operated in the village where fluid rather than fixed, context dependent rather than concrete and based on relatively content-free 'assertions of belonging or non-belonging' and assertions of the uniqueness of Elmdon. For example Strathern importantly states 'whether you are Elmdon or not Elmdon does not make a great deal of difference to ordinary everyday interaction if there are other grounds of common interest' (1982: 269). In other words community, belonging and boundary were conceptual, constituted through particular and varying forms of imagining on the part of the Elmdon residents and were context specific.

This is similar to Anthony Cohen's (1982) study of the Whalsay fishing fleet blockade in Shetland in the 1970s. The protest involving the fishermen of Whalsay – the main fishing community in Shetland – was part of national action against a series of problems such as the overfishing of Scottish waters by Icelandic, Danish and Russian fleets, the impact of cheap Norwegian frozen fish, and the imposition of fishing limit zones. In challenging conditions – of weather and politics – the Whalsay fishermen blockaded Lerwick harbour in the spring of 1975. While this was clearly on one level a collective, organic, community based action Cohen argued that 'the fleet seemed to move to the "organic" mode in its communications only when faced with outsiders – non-members – and during critical phases. So during "normal" periods the primary divisions of community and intra-community alignments were clearly evident' (1982: 298). In short what Cohen suggests is that community and social bonds were summoned up – out of particular events and sets of everyday practices – rather than simply 'existing'. For example he notes how the leader and appointed organiser of the blockade was successful in this role because he used very familiar ways of communicating with the rest of the people involved in the protest – he communicated in an ordinary way as a skipper and emphasised the values of seamanship rather than taking up a role as a community leader using a language of collective protest and solidarity. The key point to take from this is that community only emerged at particular moments and because of particular contexts and it had to be coaxed into being and it was most explicitly present only through its interactions with outsiders. However this is not to say there was no content – a number of everyday, mundane and ordinary practices and experiences could be mobilised to flesh out and make tangible the notion of community – the values and skills of seamanship; of a the shared fate; of the sense of being on the periphery of a politics and policy-making process imposed from above and from outside. The notion of boundaries and belongings being summoned up through symbols – a diverse range of rituals, customs, practices – was central to Cohen's (1985) later and highly influential text on theorising community. For Cohen it was the subjective meanings that people made out of such symbols which created notions of community rather than the existence of an objective community with quantifiable and measureable external features.

The emphasis on community as being a category for conceptual rather than concrete meaning and the emphasis on community's ability to work as a container/concealer of 'internal' social divisions – especially to those who are outside of its boundaries are themes that resonated with the project. Not least because its methodology unintentionally lent itself precisely to participants mobilising such a meta-discourse of community. There has been a tendency in rural anthropological and journalistic studies to focus in depth on a series of individuals within the case study rural areas. Ronald Blythe's study of Akenfield (1969) is perhaps the most famous of these but Nigel Rapport's (1993) study of 'Wanet' in Cumbria and Asquith's (2007) sojourn of the contemporary rural UK which was discussed earlier all follow this approach. In contrast, as Chapter 1 detailed, my project emphasised local collective conversations and interactions and its use of focus groups interviews as forums to facilitate access to these. However, this research design, in which the focus group members were all known to each other, were friends and neighbours and part of local rural networks, accentuated the outsider status of the researcher and made insider dissent difficult to be voiced and heard as the discussion of Ruth evidenced. What is possible to see from the interview extracts that I have cited from are the collectively generated expressions of anxiety and guardedness as well as revelation and intimacy.

However while the focus group method may well have lent itself to a more widely and intensely articulated 'whole community' meta-narrative it is clear that the individually focussed ethnographic immersion in a village setting does not preclude encountering the same or similar narrative as one of the key ways in which people explain and make sense of their identity and their social relationships with a particular location. One more recent example of this within rural community research has been Michael Bell's study of the Hampshire village of Childerley which I discussed in Chapter 1. As a village resident and as a social researcher Bell's study reveals the stark class based social stratifications within Childerley – he describes it as a 'slightly feudal village' in which it was possible to trace a clear divide of affluent, overwhelmingly middle class 'haves' and poorer, overwhelmingly working class 'have nots'. Bell describes the village as having 'a two-class system, Childerley is 42 per cent "have-nots" and "ordinary people" and 58 per cent "haves" and "moneyed people"' (1994: 58). Bell saw these divisions reproduced in a myriad of mundane, social practices some of which were reflected and reinforced in the use of the local pubs – the quieter and upmarket Horse and Hound pub and the noisier and much more basic Fox translated into middle class and working class residents' use.

These class divisions were apparent to Bell in other everyday habits and life style behaviours. For example Bell discusses how village residents and their families and friends using either the back door or the front door to gain entry to their houses can offer a number of cultural and class readings. Similarly the way in which gardens are designed and tended and used by their owners and the ways in which landscape and 'the view' were or were not explicitly appreciated offer insights into the social stratifications within Childerley. For example Bell observes that 'there is something about the spirit of land as landscape that feels more right to the moneyed villagers […] In other words seeing land as landscape is a bit of power trip, a metal taking possession of all one sees – something that feels right to the socially powerful' (1994: 172).

These material and class divisions and the social conflicts – most often expressed through tensions felt by working class residents as to village activities being organised and/or taken over by middle class residents – that stemmed from these were ones that were openly acknowledged by all the residents that Bell spent time with. But what is more striking is that the residents of Childerley felt uncomfortable and ambivalent about the issues of class identity and class based practices. It was the source, then, not of certainty but great unease – as Bell puts it 'while all the village residents recognize themselves as members of social classes, in general they do not feel good about it' (ibid.: 86). However, this moral ambiguity about the social stratifications in Childerley was partially resolved for the residents – middle and working class alike – by a recourse to a discourse of being more than anything, a 'country person'. Its polar opposite was being defined as a 'city person'. To belong to the category of 'country person' was a way of being bound into a broader belonging to Childerley itself. While the content of the category 'country person' is, not surprisingly, highly elusive Bell found that it required a dual commitment to a notion of local community and to a close affinity and attachment to a notion of nature. This translated into a proposition that in peaceful green settings social relations are small scale, face to face and thereby richer and more caring and able to transcend social divisions – 'there is a helpfulness in country life most villagers agreed, a unity that ties residents together across class lines' (ibid.: 92). Unlike in earlier rural community studies in Bell's study, as in mine (see Chapters 6 and 7) there is an emphasis made by participants on community *and* nature as mutually contingent and inextricably entangled categories of meaning – each brings and out reinforces the other.

That it is the *social* rather than *nature* that almost always occupies the focus of the earlier rural studies discussed here of Rees, Williams, Newby, Strathern and Cohen is particularly striking. While it is perhaps reflective of a traditional/ Enlightenment separation of nature and society and a social science treatment of nature as 'not much more than a malleable mass to be shaped at will or at the behest of cultural, economic or political forces and contestations' (Hinchliffe, 2007: 1) the ways in which notions of nature were mobilised into people's sense-making and in both the Childerley study and in my own reflect the growing attention that some of the disciplines within (and outside) social science have been paying the nature–social co-producing/hybrid/entangled relationship (for example Latour, 1999; Law, 2004; Haraway, 1991; Whatmore, 2002; Hinchliffe, 2007). However, this is not to argue that the social has become diminished in any way. As a number of commentators have noted the social – particularly when it is contained within a notion of community – has never been stronger than at the end of the 20th century and the beginning of the 21st. It is this that I now examine.

The Enduring Appeal of Community

As worries about the demise and the irretrievable loss of community abound then its appeal intensifies (Bauman, 2002). These worries are themselves part of a broader late modern social insecurity. They are worries about the loss of *particular* types of idealised communities too. This is captured in Alwyn Rees' final comments on the social changes that Llanfihangel faced. In an unequivocal indictment of urbanism he argued that,

The failure of the urban world to give its inhabitants status and significance in a functioning society, and their consequent disintegration into formless masses of rootless nonentities should make us humble in planning a new life for the countryside. The completeness of the traditional rural society – involving the cohesion of family, kindred and neighbours – and its capacity to give the individual a sense of belonging, are phenomena that might well be pondered by all who seek a better social order. (1950: 170)

This bundling of place, social ties and belonging is a potent one as I noted earlier and has become ever more potent as the communities of late modernity appear as very different to those organic, rural and working class urban ones of the past. Of course as we have seen from our discussion of Elmdon and Childerley rural communities were not quite the complete social world Rees would present. Nevertheless the discussions above testify to the importance of a notion of community that transcends conflict and division. John Clarke (2009) suggests that the yearnings about community can be understood through four popular desires: restoration, security, sociality and solidarity. Each of these are co-constitutional and convergent and each reflects and is inflected by a series of late modern anxieties and troubles – for example in using the term restoration Clarke argues that community taps into notions of a yesteryear time of more orderly social relations defined by 'proper' social conduct and social authority. Not only were social relations more mutual and warm they were also appropriately deferential and this produced a wider stability. This notion of a loss of a better way to be and behave relates to and reinforces the idea that community delivers senses of security. Late modernity's focus on the individual and corresponding decline of the state as responsible for the delivery of social well being has also been accompanied by heightened senses of vulnerability and insecurity. As the role of the welfare state has diminished in the UK and other Anglophone countries within a discourse of individual enablement, opportunity and responsibility then a general mood of risk and the unpredictability of the world have increased (Cochrane and Talbot, 2008). On our own, managing the concerns of social and economic status – un/employment, wellbeing/illness, the educational attainment of our children, old age, the fluctuations of global markets, falling and rising house prices and so forth – all add to a sense of an insecure world stalked by risk and threat. The social theorist Jock Young (2007), commenting on the disjuncture between affluent western societies and the rise in senses of insecurity within these, has described it as a kind of social vertigo – 'vertigo is the malaise of late modernity: a sense of insecurity of insubstantiality, and of uncertainty a whiff of chaos and a fear of falling.'

Young argues that living this disjuncture has resulted in a more fearful and reactionary social mood: 'the signs of giddiness, of unsteadiness, are everywhere, some serious, some minor; yet once acknowledged, a series of separate seemingly disparate facts begin to fall into place. The obsession with rules, an insistence on clear uncompromising lines of demarcation between correct and incorrect behaviour, a narrowing of borders, the decreased tolerance of deviance, a disproportionate response to rule-breaking, an easy resort to punitiveness and a point at which simple punishment begins to verge on the vindictive' (2007: 12).

In this context of social fear community has come to matter more – it becomes a form of social retreat as well as a site of socialness. The global rise of gated community living has been repeatedly been interpreted by social commentators as a form of social retreat and an attempt to securitise the everyday literally – through closed constantly monitored access – but also through an attempt to secure the social and create 'communityness' (see Blandy, 2006; Low, 2003 for example). That gated communities can be understood as both a social retreat and perversely a search for more socialness is reflected in Clarke's suggestion that the desire for sociality underpins the appeal of community. Clarke argues this sociality is not necessarily about the nostalgia of the golden age but is more about a wanting a better type of, and more transparent, social relations that goes beyond the 'alienated, calculating and mediated' forms of being together that appear to characterise early 21st-century social bonds. Clarke argues that community works as a container and model of both the imagined mutuality of an interdependent traditional sociality and a future, improved sociality.

The idea of sociality and interdependence runs through the fourth desire that Clarke suggests is part of understandings of community. This is the notion of solidarity and of shared values and concerns. This interpretation of community has been one which has been particularly drawn on as a social and survivalist resource by poor and marginalised and excluded communities. Certainly the notion of a shared fate has been one that has been applied to rural communities as we saw in the findings of Newby and agriculture workers in East Anglia and similarly in Anthony Cohen's study of the Whalsay blockade in Shetland. However, solidarity is by no means confined to the resourcefulness and bonds of the dispossessed – solidarity can be mobilised around a whole range of social issues and concerns for both the affluent middle classes as well as poorer working class populations (see Taylor, 2003 and Chapter 5 for example). The solidarity potential of communities working together to effect social change has led to the emergence of community's sister concept 'social capital' i.e. the social networks of trust and the resources that can flow from this and in part explains the centrality of community to policy making both in the UK but also more globally (Cochrane and Newman, 2009; Mooney and Neal, 2009). Just as community offers a meta-narrative which contains and glosses over social divisions and stratifications of places and locations for policy makers it has become something of a panacea for social problems and ills. In short a lot is demanded of community. In late modernity community has become even more of a 'god word' as Bell and Newby described it in 1971. It is in this vein that commentators such as Jock Young, Zygmunt Bauman and Eric Hobsbawm have all noted as the category of community becomes ever more elusive and complexly constituted in contemporary urbanist late modern societies, a traditional, straightforward, ruralist model is ever more sought after. As Hobsbawm puts it 'never was the word community used more indiscriminately and emptily than in the decades when communities in the sociological sense become hard to find in real life. Men and women look for groups to which they can belong, certainly and forever, in a world in which all else is moving and shifting, in which nothing is certain'¬ (1994: 40).

Community is a concept which makes sense to a highly diverse range of people and is one to which they *can* relate and perhaps more crucially than this it is something that a highly diverse range of people *want* to relate to. As the subsequent chapters evidence, the concept of community remains a central one in every day life and social practices. These chapters also evidence some of the troubles of the concept in everyday life and social practices but this is inevitable. Even in the warm glow of Llanfihangel Alwyn Rees was already troubled by the shadows and shifts that he saw as increasing as the effects of mobility and urbanism continued their long reach. Just as gated communities seem to reflect people's desire to belong, albeit within a highly constructed and securitised community which is completely contingent on keeping most others out, so too can counter urbanisation migrations be explained in part by the desire to find and then become part of an organic, small scale, caring, interdependent local community – and, in England, with its dominant national narrative of pastoralism this seems more likely to be found within rural environments than urban ones (Strathern, 1982; Bell, 1994).

People actively in search of community tend to be committed to its visibility and to making it visible and expend effort and imagination into this task. In rural areas this tends to follow some of the stratifications we have noted earlier. While in Lanfihangel the sociality that Clarke describes was of the hearth and home, between neighbours and kin, even here this was giving way to more self-consciously constructed social bonds. In contemporary rural settings visible community tends to be actualised by the self conscious community-creating efforts of 'busy' individuals, social and leisure organisations, interest groups, the church and so forth (see Chapters 5, 6 and 7). Both Strathern and Bell observed community-making labours in Elmdon and Childerley and both noted the irony that the efforts to create community through mainly middle class driven activities of organising the village fete, the harvest festival, the tidying up of the village graveyard and so on, actually led to new divisions and resentments and senses of local customs and concerns being taken over by those moving into the village from outside. But in many ways it is these efforts to *make* community that are important. It is too easy to accuse community of being a strawman but then not account for its popularity and social appeal. That people do yearn for and expend considerable effort in actualising community does need to be attended to and acknowledged. We can note its silencing of internal dissent and difference and we can note its inevitable boundary construction and its highly problematic constant excluding and including dynamic but for me it is the appeal of community that remains crucial to keep in mind. We cannot simply dismiss the search for and construction of community as parochial, inward looking, reactionary and defensive practices – although these may indeed each or all be part of community-making processes too – as Jock Young puts it 'the building of community, its invention, becomes that of a narrative which celebrates and embraces one side and vilifies and excludes on the other' (2007: 128). But my suggestion is that that is only a partial story of community. Similarly only partially accurate is the narrative that community is continually elusive and never more so in the current era of precariousness and uncertainty.

Perhaps there is another, slighter or thinner but nevertheless still compelling social story which takes into account community's ability to transcend difference and division. Jock Young compares organic communities with late modern ones and notes that the former were face to face, intergenerational, embedded in locality and local identity and informal processes of social control. He argues that, in contrast, the features of later modern communities are difference, fragmentation, pluralism and transience. They are mediated, global, calculating and chaotic in that wealth and poverty can exist cheek by jowl. And yet for all this there does remain a sociality. Young is speaking of community in urban settings. But what happens if we apply his model to rural settings? Would it be so different? It would be possible to suggest that communities both in early and late modern settings were more convergent of the features identified in Young's two lists. Cheek by jowl wealth and poverty were very much features of rural settlement. Transient and mobile populations have also been much more part of rural environments than popularly assumed. Not only because of some of the social changes of enclosure and clearance and changes in agricultural production but because agriculture itself has always required labour on intermittent and seasonal basis – agriculture has a tradition of using low paid migrant labour which it maintains today. The organic communities of the past, whether as the rural model or the industrial working class based model, were more mobile, divided, heterogeneous and chaotic than they are now recalled as being. Similarly my suggestion here is that the fragmented, pluralist, mediated, late modern communities are not completely without a social dimension or face to face interaction or a local identity or senses of belonging being expressed by those that live in those localities.

The current policy and political interest in social capital reflects some of this aspect of social relations in both urban and rural settings. For example Anne Power and Helen Willmot's (2007) study of poor urban areas in the North of England and in the East End of London found practices and social relations that had 'organic' – i.e. social trust and mutual bonds – dimensions to them. The study, conducted over an eight year period, tracked 200 families and sought to examine how the conditions of an area impacted on the formation or depletion of social capital. Power and Willmot found that their respondents talked extensively about community, social networks, family relations and supports within all four areas.

The vast majority of respondents felt they had people to count on and to turn to and most commonly these were family, friends and/or neighbours. Family contact and support was common amongst respondents especially in the North England area and especially around child care and support. Most friends were locally based and 60 per cent of respondents have at least weekly contact with their friends who were a source of practical and emotional support. The majority of respondents' accounts revealed a high level of trust in their relationships with their neighbours.

Similarly, in their study into the ways in which contemporary 'social patterns and process in small rural places help to produce distinctive bases for social identities and social cohesion' Malcolm Mosley and Ray Pahl (2007: 3) found – to greater and lesser extents – 'organic' community dimensions in all four of their rural case study areas. For example in one Shropshire rural town Bishops Castle – Mosley and Pahl argue that there was a remarkable bonding that had developed between 'ordinary people' keen to take forward the annual organisation of a dozen or so festivities of various kinds (2007: 23). In a direct echo of Rees' Llanfihangel findings – and to which I return to later – Moseley and Pahl also emphasised the importance of the convivial and the informal: 'The key feature [of successful social capital] is informality based on trust; people seem to come together and get on with tasks with little or no formal organisation in the accepted sense' (ibid.).

My point is a simple one. It is that some caution is needed so as not to overstate linearity of the organic to fragmented community story. While late modern perceptions and experiences of risk and uncertainty and precariousness have produced heightened senses of ontological insecurity which have driven in part the desires for community and the rural community model in particular it is important to not fall into the trick of the god word of community nor over imagine both its yesteryear glow and its contemporary decline.

Conclusion

I began this chapter by noting that the concept of community was difficult but ubiquitous. As Susanne MacGregor (2003) has suggested it is something of a 'weasel word' in that it is able to hold and accommodate a range of meanings and practices. While I pick up again on the troubles of community and its much argued over status in Chapter 5 it is the ways in which community continues to have meaning and importance to people outside of the worries of social science and the ways in which community has been a focus of for rural studies research that has been central to this chapter. I have suggested that community appears to grow in importance rather than decline. The search for community reflects the uncertainty of what Richard Sennet (1998) calls the 'new capitalism' of the western/global north. The rural community in particular acts as a condensation symbol in that it is able to summon up notions of the organic, the small scale, the local, social well-being, trust and mutuality. The chapter has argued that the examples of studies of rural communities reveal a rather more complex picture of mutuality and highly stratified patterns of social relations. These studies also provided insights to the ways in which community does not simply exist as a constant, observable thing but rather is summoned up according to context and event and threat – it becomes known only through its interactions with others and often those others are outsiders. In being summoned up in these different moments and ways community is able to hold contradictory properties by making a purchase on place and locality and the rural. We saw some of this with Ruth in the Appleby conversation retreat from an assertion of class differences in the village and we saw it in Bell's Childerley and in Strathern's Elmdon and Newby's East Anglia.

Despite its largely symbolic and 'of the mind' rather than concrete existence the seductions of community go beyond an abstract appeal or claim and does translate into enacted social practices – some small everyday acts of mutuality and trust; others progressive and others defensive. I have argued that there is not an unbroken story of a once existing organic rural community-ness to a contemporary anomic urban non-community. This, and the extent to which people commit themselves to assembling and maintaining structures of community feeling, is examined and taken further in Chapter 5. However this raises the question as to where such community making processes stem from? While I have suggested that contemporary ontological insecurities and Clarke's four optics explain the fantasy of community these do not *wholly* account for the enduring appeal and mobilisation of the rural community. As Strathern concludes in her study of Elmdon, 'I have not in the end been able to explain why the *village* as such is a potent source of symbolism' (1982: 274. Original emphasis). What I want to rather tentatively propose is that the focus on the *social* of the studies of rural communities obscured the ways in which their very *spatiality* impacts on notions of belonging and attachment and affection. Bell's Childerley apart there is a strange absence of rural nature and of ethnicity in these studies. What happens when we incorporate rural nature and nation to the category community? It is this question that the next chapter attempts to think through.

Chapter 4
Rethinking Rurality:
Ethnicity and Englishness

Introduction

What is meant by ethnicity? How can the relationship between ethnicity, community and space be understood? In what ways is each contingent and how does each constitute the other? Is ethnicity solely a social and culturally based concept? It is these kinds of questions which this chapter attempts to think through. But I want to begin with a vignette. In June 2008 the Hayward Gallery hosted the Psycho Buildings exhibition – a stunning and strange collection of installations in which the physical and emotional collided in a range of disorientating and reassuring ways. While the little boating lake installed on the very top of the gallery itself held a particular appeal and attracted a long queue it was Rachel Whiteread's installation 'Place (Village) 2006–2008' which was a collection of 20 or so terraced dolls houses all lit up in a darkened room that most affected me. It reminded me of driving home as a child in winter evenings back to our outlying farm on the moors and leaving behind Hebden Bridge, cosy in its deep valley, and seeing the little town grow smaller and more twinkly with its warm bright lights clustered at the centre and straggling up the hillsides before giving way to the emptiness of the fields and moors. And it reminded me of more recent holidays in rural Italy and looking across from cooling terraces to the shadowy mountain views on darkening evenings and seeing the tiny, far off lights of other hamlets and villages breaking up those dark wooded expanses. There is a comfort to be taken in the sight of those little human habitations with their associations of home/s and dwelling. Being enchanted by the Rachel Whiteread houses (and minimising their ambiguity – when you look closely the houses are all eerily empty) I suddenly recalled some of the conversations from the focus group interviews on the idea of home which resonated with my own reactions to Whiteread's dolls houses:

> Penny: Just here [the village] is very pretty.
>
> Lesley: Oh yes.
>
> Pip: Oh yes, this green and everything.
>
> Penny: With the thatched cottages.
>
> Jan: Now we've opened up the church you know, that is what, actually that is quite a nice, when you walk up at night, when the lights are on in the church and

its coming shining out through the window, although it's dark you've got this light shining.

Penny: And what I love is that they've got the clock chiming again.

Jan: Oh yes. [lots of murmurs of agreement]

Penny: And that's what I like, that's country life. (Appleby WI)

Researcher: Do you have a favourite place or view or building or something that is special to you?

Marion: […] I just like the view from our windows. We can see a long way in front and a long way at the back. Just fields and trees and lights in the distance at night, that's nice and it's comforting to see the lights. (Little Buckley WI)

The personal and the picturesque; the green; buildings, light and dark; the social and sounds are all being bundled together here as defining senses of reassurance, home and of 'country life'. But these notions and perceptions of home and comfort tap directly into broader contexts of familiarity and belonging. Brian Short has suggested 'if the word "rural" has its own aura, so too does "community". Put the two together and the effect is to multiply the mythology to something more than the sum of its constituent parts. Add "English" and the effect is like a chemical chain reaction which grows and glows, subfusing everything in a good green light' (1992: 4). There is something of Short's 'good, green light' in the Appleby conversation and in Marion's comments and in my own accounts of the reassurances of seeing the lit up houses on various hillsides.

Home, as Les Back (2007) reminds us, has very different associations. Citing John Berger, Back emphasises the diverse meanings of home – it encompasses domestic morality, property and family and extends out to notions of the homeland, nation and patriotism. But, Back and Berger remind us, 'there is an antecedent meaning…home is the centre of the world – not in a geographical, but in an ontological sense…the place from which the world can be founded' (Back: 2007: 69). It is the multidimensional meanings of home and security that also lie in David Matlass' suggestion that the 'nucleated English village tends to have a focus, often the church, physically, historically and emotionally at the core' (1994: 77) and it is this that can be heard here in Ida's comment about the church, village and home:

It's the community around the church and a lot of people, we had a funeral in the village a few weeks ago, a real village character, and the whole village turned out. There was standing room only in the church and I was talking to the widow afterwards at the wake in the pub and she said 'when my children come along the A431 and they turn off and they see the church they know they're home'. Because it sticks up…and it is not necessarily like that for people who attend church...but the actual physical presence of the building means the village for me. (Ida, Farleigh WI)

The villagescape described here by Ida and the one described in the Appleby conversation are able to call on a sense of Englishness without any reference to the nation-state itself. The summoning of nation in this way comes through what Billig (1992) has identified as a 'banal' or everyday framework of hailing national belonging and assembling a majoritised ethnic identity.

In this rather round about way then I have begun to describe the task this chapter will set itself – understanding the processes whereby a particular ethnic identity constantly slips between interior and exterior worlds; between different scales of home; between the individual and the notion of national belonging. Divided into two broad parts the first section of this chapter addresses some of the thinking on what constitutes ethnicity and the second section focuses on the notion of Englishness as an ethnic identity and asks what gets called upon and folded into its formations.

Ethnicity: Formations of Personal, Social and National Identity – When are they Ethnic?

I began this chapter by talking of notions of what we recognise and know and what gives us sense of home and familiarity and comfort – i.e. a process of confirming ontological security. In lights and buildings and sounds perceptions of culture are being mobilised as central components in this process of confirming identity and belonging. But it is worth remembering from the previous chapter that securitisation of identity stems from a wider perception of precariousness. Just as community becomes a desired concept with which to 'hold chaos in abeyance' (Young, 1999) so too notions of culture and cultural differences which we recognise and of which we are part (or don't recognise and of which we are not part) may be used in the same way.

I noted in the previous chapter that some of the value of the early rural community studies research lay in the ways in which they represented the casting of the anthropological gaze onto the 'familiar' communities of 'home' rather than the 'exotic' communities of 'other' places. This has been a particular trouble – amongst a rather long list of troubles – with the category 'ethnic'. In a range of everyday, political, policy and social science contexts it is overwhelmingly associated with and used to define the cultural content and practices of the other or of minoritised populations rather than majoritised populations. It is an acceptable long hand for the rather less acceptable short hand of the cultural 'them and us'. In this way majoritised cultures are *de-ethnicised* and instead take on a status as 'the norm' against which other cultures are compared and explicitly ethnicised – either negatively or positively. Majority culture is not conceived of through the optic of ethnicity. As Mairtin Mac an Ghaill (1999: 41) puts it,

> An under-explored set of questions emerges from an English/British ethnic majority identity position, concerning a collective national past and future. Who are 'we'? Who were 'we'? Who have 'we' become? Who can 'we' become? Social and cultural theorists have concentrated too much on the exclusions of those positioned as subordinate, such as ethnic minorities. Presently there is a need to begin to develop frameworks that explore the changing collective self-representations of dominant forms of Anglo-ethnicity and the accompanying material and symbolic systems and practices that produce this ethnicity that is not named as such.

Despite the flurry of books mentioned in earlier chapters and their antecedents – Paxman's (1998) *The English* and Scruton's (2000) *England: An Elegy* for example – these do not speak to Mac an Ghaill's urging of the scrutiny of an 'ethnicity that is not named as such' but rather speak of a deep unease about the meanings of and changes in Englishness and Britishness and sense of crisis about, as Vron Ware describes it, 'national identity and the identity of the nation' (2007: 2). As I write this I look at the covers of these texts lying on my desk. Scruton's book shows a blurred picture of an Edwardian dressed couple on a beach with a white cliff in the background and a little (maybe a Fox Terrier?) dog in the foreground. Paxman's cover has an 18th-century sketch of John Bull devouring French galleon ships and a bottle labelled 'true British stout' at his feet. In other words these are images which conjure up familiar and fantasy symbols which allude to the nation state, national identity, historical memories and historical forgettings, a political and a cultural territory as much as a geographical one.

The constant bleed between ethnic identity and national identity is an unsurprising one given their co-constitutive relationship. Nations draw heavily on ideas of shared culture, kinship, history and ethnic identity is not without geography – ethnicity relies on ideas of having ties to real and imagined homelands. Nevertheless these categories are not completely collapsible into the other. One is ostensibly about politics and the other is about culture. However, such delineations are not easily drawn and marked out in social relations. Each may borrow from itself to reinforce the other. Each works with notions of being natural and a given rather than being assembled and manufactured. The political/cultural distinction has been used to establish discourses of political hegemony – national identity has been one that has been mobilised in order to describe majoritised populations whereas ethnicity has been mobilised in order to describe minoritised, subordinated populations, for example. In the context of England the national narrative is both quiet *and* noisy. Michael Billig argues that nationalism has received most attention in its extreme and 'thickly' politicised forms. Billig's argument, of which mine around ethnicity can be understood as an extension, is that it is important to attend to the ways in which nationalism and national identity operate in 'low level' everyday and 'banal' ways and so continually remind us of and allow us to interpret our sense of national belonging. Billig argues that 'national identity in established nations is remembered because it is embedded in routines of life, which constantly "remind", or "flag", nationhood. However, these reminders or "flaggings", are so numerous and are such a familiar part of the social environment, that they operate mindlessly, rather than mindfully' (1995: 38).

Gargi Battacharyya has argued that identity presents similar challenges and that identities are 'most clearly marked for those who in some way inhabited the margins of society. The powerful (all those infamous straight white class privileged and able-bodied men) seemed to have hardly any identity at all' (1999: 81). It is significant that Battacharyya lists whiteness here because studies of whiteness too have laboured to excavate and define the meanings and social practices of whiteness away from the obvious site of white supremacist politics (Frankenberg, 1992; 1997; Ware, 1992; Dyer, 1997; Neal, 1995; 1998). I have suggested that the categories of nationalism, identity, whiteness and ethnicity share the same challenges when they are mapped onto cartographies of powerfulness. All of these are categories that are proximate and relational. They melt into and sustain each other. It is no surprise that majoritised ethnicity works in the same way – so while minoritised ethnicity is continually flagged and marked out as distinct and separate, majoritised ethnicity works as unremarkable and ubiquitous and in this way presents as normative and thereby dominant. It is not seen as 'ethnic' but rather as a cultural given, as culturally universalist. In this way saris are ethnic but twinsets not. Gulab jamun is ethnic but jam roly-poly not.

These are rather light-hearted examples of course but they do work to starkly illustrate 'us' and 'them' formations and processes of ethnic identification. In this context there is a need to *de-nationalise* Englishness and ethnicise it instead. Despite this I am slightly hesitant about making claims for recognising Englishness as an ethnic identity as it feels as though I maybe skirting rather close to concretising and privileging the cultural hegemony of Englishness and its associated, spurious claims of cultural superiority which have, alongside biological concepts of race, been at the heart of the colonial project and which continue to inform and inflect many contemporary discourses of Englishness. The troubles associated with the concept of ethnicity are reflected in the academic arguments as to its meaning and impacts on contemporary social relations. It is these that are now considered.

Ethnicity: A Category in Ascendancy in a Local–Global World

I have suggested that ethnicity may be best understood through the interactions of culture, identity and social relations and more specifically cultural difference and social-cultural practices. Frederick Barth (1969) explained ethnicity as the 'social organisation of cultural difference' and Clifford Geertz (1973) as 'the world of personal identity collectively ratified and publicly expressed'. Stressing the connectivity between the interior worlds of individuals and the exterior social environments Richard Jenkins (1999: 88) identifies four key elements in the useful 'basic model' that he offers for defining ethnicity:

- Ethnicity is about cultural differentation;
- Although ethnicity is centrally concerned with culture it is also rooted in, and to some extent the outcome of, social interaction;
- Ethnicity is no more fixed or unchanging than the culture of which it is a component;
- Ethnicity is a social identity which is both collective and individual, externalised in social interaction and internalised in personal self-awareness.

Jenkins' model rightly places its emphasis on the centrality of the social but also on the inherent instabilities of ethnic identification. But, what Jenkins' model understates is the place of emotion and what Fenton calls the 'intensity' of ethnic identification and sentiment (1999: 92). The addition of emotion is one that this chapter suggests is necessary in the analysis of ethnicity. Not only is it a labile category but ethnicity has a relatively recent history in academic study and the wider social world. It has only really emerged out of anthropology and into broader social science, political and policy usage since the late 1960s. Indeed as recently as 1975 Nathan Glazer and Daniel Moynihan described ethnicity as a 'new term' in their influential edited collection *Ethnicity: Theory and Evidence.* The actual roots of the term ethnic go back to older related usage – notably the Greek *ethnos* – which Hutchinson and Smith (1996) note is found used to refer to a band of friends or tribe. However, the ascendancy of ethnicity into mainstream everyday and political discourse in the last quarter of the 20th and beginning of the 21st century can be understood as the result of a number of contributing factors. These include increasing linkages between ethnicity and discourses of race and race relations (Banton, 1983; 1987 and see Chapter 7); the post cold war reordering and the (often violent) re/emergence of new nation states and ethnic centred conflict within these; perceptions of globalisation and uncertainty. I want to focus on the latter for the time being.

When perceptions of uncertainty and change are strong then the process of calling on an ethnic identity may be more acute. Like community, ethnicity appears to offer a set of shared bonds that precedes the political turbulence that throws up new nations and buries old ones. Like community, ethnicity has pre-modern and almost organic associations. Like community, ethnic identity can offer senses of ontological certainty and reassurance in the face of insecurity and change. As Daniel Bell has argued:

Ethnicity has become more salient because it can combine an interest with an affective tie. Ethnicity provides a tangible set of common identifications – in language, food, music, names – when other social roles become more abstract and impersonal. In the competition for the values of the society to be realised politically, ethnicity can become a means of claiming place or advantage [...] In trying to account for the upsurge in ethnicity today, one can see this ethnicity as the emergent expression of primordial feelings long suppressed but now awakened, or as a new mode of seeking political redress in the society. (1975 cited in Hutchinson and Smith, 1996: 144)

In the three decades that have passed since Bell made this observation the salience of ethnicity has become even more marked and the processes of globalisation have in part shaped some of this.

There is now an extensive set of debates surrounding the concept and phenomenon of globalisation that I need not rehearse here (see Beck, 2000; Savage et al., 2005; Davies, 2005; Young, 2007). However, while there has undoubtedly been an increase in the degrees and types of connectivity in the world as a result of economic restructuring, political reordering, trans and international companies and organisations, multiculture, continuing migrations, technological communications, cheap air travel and so forth, this has not subsumed or diminished nation states or ushered in a monolithic, corporate culture. In many ways it has done the opposite as populations have increasingly looked to notions of ethnicity and nationhood as ways of creating or maintaining ontological certainties. As globalisation commentators have noted it makes more sense to see globalisation as working in an iterative and recursive way with local spaces and places rather than as an irresistible and flattening process (see Clarke, 2005 for example). As Ulrich Beck puts it 'globalisation is a non linear, dialectic process in which the global and the local do not exist as cultural polarities but as combined and mutually implicating principles' (2002: 17). While the acknowledgement of the multidirectional nature of the relationship between the local and global allows room for thinking through the ways in which populations make sense of 'who they are' and 'what they know', this leaves the troubling question as to what the local is rather unanswered. Is the local the interior world of individuals, home, neighbourhood, locality, community, landscape, nation? (Savage et al., 2005.) While it may seem rather facile to suggest that there is something of all of these constantly if unevenly at play in the notion of the local it is nevertheless important to be able to work across these dimensions and highlight the imagined and concrete interactions and connectivities between the personal and the place. Holding on to the importance of territory within this is emphasised by Savage et al. and they point to the importance of Bourdieu's concepts of habitus and field as these allow a dual focus on the profound connectivities between peoples' senses of social and spatial comfort. This multiscale relationship between the person and the experiences and sense making of the locales that they inhabit is very much present in this extract of a WI focus group conversation:

Researcher: Tell me about your favourite places or your favourite views.

Susie: I love our church. I'm so pleased we have a church.

Researcher: Tell me about the church.

Susie: I think it's a lovely little church isn't it? I don't know…I just feel this, this sort of/

Irene: It belongs to you.

Susie: /an affiliation to it […] and because I've lived in funny places and haven't been able to go to church for a long time because they've either been Muslim or whatever I haven't been able to practice anything so its really rather nice to have somewhere to go and again that is a real feeling of community, to go somewhere once a week and see everybody and feel like you're joining in something. I'm actually a Catholic so I'm not Church of England, but it doesn't matter that's what's so lovely […] it doesn't matter what you are come anyway.

Irene: We had that woman in the black thing the other week didn't we?

Susie: […] I just think that its lovely and when I go there and do the flowers, you're on your own, and it's just somewhere nice to be.

Jean: […] yes there is something about the church/

Sylvia: because it's not huge and we've got lovely windows/

Rachel: and there's a feeling about it.

[…]

Jan: And it tells a history as well.

There are a number of things at work here which veer between the expressions of appreciative feelings – the repeated description of the church and of being within it as 'lovely' and 'nice' and of it being open and inclusive – and expressions of unease and reassurance. These are seen for example in Susie's descriptions of living in 'funny places' feeling 'out of place' in these and contrasting these with the emphasis on community, belonging, weekly routines and familiarity. Other examples of this unease are visible in Irene's (unresponded to) reminder to the group of the proximity of cultural difference and Jan's allusion to buildings being able to work as symbols and repositories of the past. While there are these multiple strands of inter-relating of dialogue and sense making going on in this piece of conversation my main point is to demonstrate the ability to move from interior to exterior worlds without apparent disjunctures.

This is also demonstrated in the contribution made by Chris in the one of Northumberland Young Farmers focus group interviews when he is describing what he feels when he stops for a minute and thinks about where he lives: 'if you stand and again and look at the view that we've got and you see the trees and the moors and the land, the free land, you think that's it, you're in England' (cited in

Neal and Agyeman, 2006: 3). The way in which Chris moves here from his view of his local landscape to being able to have a sense of being in England and to national belonging is a process that this chapter returns to and which is taken up later in the book (see Chapter 7 for example), but it is sufficient to note at this point the process through which Englishness is assembled via the non-human. The assemblage affords comfort too – Chris emphasises that when you see this view you are 'in' England and that it is 'free land'. What gets gathered up and assigned particular social, cultural and political meanings reflects an interaction between individuals and the(ir) surrounds or landscapes in which they live. The ways in which the particular versions of rural England get called upon for comfort and reassurance at times of anxiety, threat, insecurity and danger has received increasing attention (see Chapters 1 and 2 and Williams, 1976; Wright, 1984; Sibley, 1997; Neal, 2002 for example). This process of calling on rural England for securing the nation is not new of course and can be seen in Stanley Baldwin's 1924 description of the sounds and sights of rural Worcestershire (Wright, 1982; 2008 and see below) and runs through to William Whitelaw's description of his view from his garden during the urban unrest in London in 1982:

> Sitting out after supper on a beautiful hot summer evening, looking at the fields and trees of Burnham Beeches. It was a perfect, peaceful English scene. Was it really the same country as the riot towns and cities which I had visited that week? Was it really in the same vicinity as parts of London a few miles away which were at that moment full of troubles? Surely, I thought, this peaceful countryside represents more accurately the character and mood of the vast majority of the British people. (Whitelaw, 1989, cited in Neal, 2002: 445)

It is there too in John Major's unplayful 1992 allusions to George Orwell's playful list of markers of Englishness and of course it is there too in populist discourse disseminated in rural lifestyle magazines such as *Country Living* which regularly feature the voices of people for whom rural England works as a container of both ethnic identification and security, as this interview with a local police officer illustrates:

> There is a real feeling of history here, among the ruined castles and scattered villages, *a sense of England you don't get any more in cities.* I know it's remarkable but I think *we get less crime now* than ten years ago. There hasn't been a murder since I came here [25 years ago] and we get a serious assault, a drunken brawl that's got out of hand, only once or twice a year. West Hereford must be one of the *safest* places in England. We have a minor but growing problem of drugs among the young. If something happens in the cities it'll happen here eventually. Domestic burglary averages three a month, mostly committed by criminals *travelling here from cities.* (cited in Neal, 2002: 446. Emphasis added)

As Wright argues there is no need for a 'palpable threat' to Englishness, such as war, to effectively conjure up Englishness as precarious and perilously threatened: 'even in peace time, being English can feel like a perpetual Dunkirk, in which everything that is valued is polarised against encroaching developments that promise only nullification and destruction' (2008 www.patrickwright.co.uk).

Certainly the idea of Englishness as being in a precarious position increases in the face of the perception of ever increasing and homogenising global connectivities. Indeed the worries of commentators like Kingsnorth discussed in Chapter 1 testify to the sense of the endangerment to cultural, national and ethnic identities – 'the English, perhaps uniquely among European nations, are becoming almost a de-cultured people' (Kingsnorth, 2007: 283). Similarly for Scruton 'when your fundamental loyalty is to a place and its *genius loci*, globalisation and the loss of sovereignty bring a crisis of identity. The land loses its history and its personal face […] it has induced in the English the sense that they are really living nowhere' (2000: 246). In this way, in the iterative and recursive local–global relationship, the local – in its broadest sense – can and often does become re-emphasised and valorised. For Kingsnorth the local and Englishness are endlessly folded into the other and it is a 'commitment to place and to culture [that] can provide a bulwark against the advance of the global consumer machine' (ibid.: 15). While the link between place and culture in itself is not problematic it does become so when it conceived of as a defensive partnership as the notion of a 'bulwark' implies here. Indeed the notion of the assertion of Englishness as a defensive identity runs through the position articulated by Kingsnorth and others. This tendency inflects my own unease in my argument to perform a 360 degree move away the idea of nationhood in Englishness and focus instead on it as an assembled ethnic identity. Being in sympathy with Paul Gilroy's urging of a '"post ethnic" global humanism' (2004: 167) my use of the term 'assembled' here is very deliberate because it clearly flags the social basis of ethnicity. However, the emotional intensity of ethnic formations cannot be neglected. This is both because this emotionalism requires analysis and because of the ways in which the idea of the primordial that has been drawn on as a way of explaining this intensity (Jenkins, 1997; Fenton, 1999). It is this that I now want to consider.

Ethnicity: Representations and Mobilisations of the Primordial?

The role of the primordial with formations of ethnicity has been a focus of extended debate within anthropology and ethnicity and race studies (Geertz, 1973; Barth, 1969; 1994; Banton, 1983; Rex and Mason, 1986; Jenkins, 1997; Fenton, 1999). The primordial refers to an idea of a fixed and unchanging ethnic identity that is rooted in notions of kinship and place and language and culture and history – in its most basic conceptualisation it can be understood as 'born and bred' ethnic identity. While this focus on the primordial has been contrasted with the situational or instrumental arguments that ethnicity is a social product that is fluid and context specific, Jenkins (1997) has suggested that the polarity between these and their associated theorists, Clifford Geertz and Frederick Barth, has been overstated. As Jenkins points out, the two positions actually share much common ground. Jenkins argues that Geertz acknowledged the importance of culture and its ability to change over space and time and Barth acknowledged that ethnic formations contain a stability to them which means that ethnic identities *may* change not that they *inevitably* do. Sandra Wallman (1986: 230) also argues that Barth's well known metaphor of ethnicity being a 'vessel' of (and for) boundary construction which is sometimes empty and sometimes full but 'always there' is suggestive of the primordial. There is a general social science consensus – based on theoretical argument and ethnographic research – that the 'pure' primordial view of ethnicity is generally inaccurate and speaks mostly to commonsense understandings of ethnicity. As Gargi Bhattacharyya argues we have moved away from ideas of 'ethnicity as a negative determination – instead of being seen as a fixed (and often painful) legacy which you inherit, ethnicity comes to be seen as another *strategic performance*, something which you stage in everyday life according to circumstances, using a variety of repertoires which might include a version of the traditional as well as the influences of the new context' (1997: 81. Emphasis added).

However, what is relevant to my discussions is the extent to which notions of a primordially framed ethnicity dominate the more everyday conceptualisations of ethnic identity. This reflects the duality of the individual/private and collective/public dimensions through which ethnicity is subscribed to. In other words because ethnicity partially works through attachments and affections and familiarities and recognition then the emotional has to be incorporated into considerations of the ways in which ethnicity becomes performed and mobilised. The fieldwork data already cited in this chapter testify that it is 'feelings' and 'the personal' that most dominate the interactions between individuals and the wider worlds they inhabit. Again Jenkins makes the important contribution that we 'need to acknowledge affect and emotion in our considerations of ethnicity […] but there is, it must be said no necessary contradiction between instrumental manipulation on the one hand and sentiment, on the other. They may actually go hand in hand' (1997: 90).

It is precisely ethnicity's ability to work in and through emotional registers which means that the *idea* of the primordial needs to be focussed on in the examination of processes of formations of ethnicity. There is for example a sense of the primordial in Raymond Williams' description of his relationship to where he grew up and the notion of home:

> Around the idea of settlement…a real structure of values has grown. It draws on
> many deep and persistent feelings: identification with the people among whom
> we grew up: an attachment to the place, the landscape in which we first lived

and learned to see. I know these feelings at once, from my own experience. The only landscape I ever see, in dreams, is the Black Mountain village in which I was born. When I go back...I feel a recovery of a particular kind of life...and inescapable identity...a positive connection. (1979: 106)

Reading this account of Williams' bond with the place where he grew up reminded me of reading about Ted Hughes describing West Yorkshire and the Pennine hills around the village of Heptonstall as being his 'tuning fork'. These descriptions speak of geographical attachments that can become deeply established between people and the places in which they inhabit and the ways in which emotions 'are intimately tied into place' (Urry, 2005: 77). This is why the primordial dimension of ethnicity cannot be discounted as it reflects two key aspects of ethnic identity. First, as we have discussed above, the personal and the emotional are particularly profound and so lend themselves to being experienced and viewed through the optic of the primordial – these are the emotions that make us feel un/comfortable and in/secure. It can be difficult to articulate and express emotions and the basis and reasons for them so they tend to appear stay at that primordial 'instinctive' level. Again if we look back at some of the project's data in this chapter this is very visible. There is a visceral dimension to these conversations – 'it feels nice', 'it means home', 'it's just lovely' and so forth. Because it *feels* visceral does not mean that it *is* visceral but it does mean that the emotions that make it feel as though it is visceral need to be attended to more than they generally have been in academic analysis (Bondi et al., 2005).

Second, the foregrounding of the primordial gives ethnicity its inherited, passed on, born into, *given* character. In the same way that 'race science' drew heavily on a discourse of biology as a social process (see Chapter 7 for more discussion of the relationship between race and ethnicity) representations of ethnicity as primordial allows the cultural and the social components that make up ethnicity to be naturalised. It is possible to see the primordial being continually being folded into discourses of unease about contemporary rural England and endangered Englishness. For example a return to just the title of the Kingsnorth text *Real England* evidences this in that it works with notions of an ethnic and national identity as fixed, fundamental, profound, organic. This reading of an 'organic' ethnic identity threads itself across the chapters of the book as Kingsnorth tells us that 'as the globalised, placeless world spreads [...] it could be that the most radical thing to do is belong. Belonging is a human need [...] we need to be part of something. Yet true belonging surely needs a place as well as people. It means belonging to a piece of land, a community – and being prepared to defend it' (2007: 16). Askwith too tells us that 'I imagined rural England and had blithely gone through life (eagerly embracing the modern whenever I found it) under the impression that it would always be there, like a great rock, with the past clinging to it like lichen. Now, when I turn to look at it, it was gone' (2007: 7). Slightly preceding both of these but speaking in very similar terms in his lament for an

England changed beyond recognition Roger Scruton explains how although the 'physical country remains its landscape has gone' and tells of how 'his father loved what was local, collegial and attached to the land [...] deep down his passion was a religious one, a protest against a world which placed material prosperity before spiritual need, and which ignored the fact that the soul of a man is a local product, rooted in the soil' (2000: 256).

The primordial runs through these accounts in various inter-related ways. It is expressed as the physical world and the theme of profound ties to the land, to the soil, rocks. It is there too in Scruton's deployment of kinship through his discussion of his father's relationship to Englishness. It is there too in the idea of a sense of belonging to a community and to a local – a local that may need to be 'defended' and to the idea of people as being 'local products'.

It is not the emotion of the attachment but the *representation* of it as being *beyond* the social that is troubling. As I noted earlier belonging and the establishment of an affectionate relationship with the landscapes with which we are familiar is part of the identity processes we all engage in to feel at ease and comfortable. My reaction to Rachael Whiteread's dolls houses reflects the ways in which external landscapes are able to bind them to us. But this occurs as a social and emotional not as a primal and instinctive process. In Chapter 7 I will return to this idea of building attachments to landscapes and will draw on Savage et al.'s (2005) concept of elective belonging, which captures the process by which people chose to become attached and develop their ties to place and locality. There is no requirement to have been born in that place or to have a long generational reach back into the localised past to develop a sense of home and belonging and place of affection. As Savage et al. put it 'elective belonging involves people moving to a place and putting down roots. [...] people feel they belong when they are able to biographically make sense of their decision to move to a particular place and their sense of belonging is hence linked to the contingent tie between themselves and their surrounds' (2005: 207). It is the *elective* part of the concept that is crucial as it flags agency and the social rather than structures and the primordial. It also highlights openness in terms of identity formations, place attachment and senses of belonging as opposed to essentialised rather than closed and defensive boundaries.

The differences between these opposite positions represent what Sandra Wallman has called the 'ethnic double bind' (1986: 231); by which she means that the more permeable and relaxed an ethnic boundary then the greater the possibility for change but the less strain there is on that identity. Conversely the more policed and defensive the boundary then the more unlikely it will be to change and develop, even if its 'integrity' is more likely to be preserved. In her ethnographic research into two multiethnic (then) solidly working class boroughs of inner London Wallman found both of these approaches in evidence. Wallman contrasts the between differences the more heterogeneous and open Battersea in South London and the more homogenous and closed Bow in East London. Arguing that the jobs, housing, gatekeepers and political traditions of each area played a critical role in establishing the open or closedness of the ethnic boundary in these parts of London Wallman concludes that 'membership in the Battersea area seems to be possible as long as you behave like a local: an incomer can become a local person just by moving in, behaving appropriately and staying around. Membership in the Bow area, in line with East End tradition, is not so readily achieved. It is ascribed by birth, or perhaps by marriage, but generally it is much more difficult to become "local" in the East End than in South London' (1986: 240–1). From this Wallman suggests that localism is stronger in Battersea and, while belonging is conditional, belonging is possible. There is something of Savage et al.'s elective belonging concept at work in Wallman's interpretations of Battersea's porous boundary. However she argues that in Bow it is ethnic principles that prevail. Ethnic principles that are primordially cast mean that the possibilities of and potential for belonging are much more difficult and challenging as the boundaries are being reinforced and maintained.

Englishness: A Defensive Ethnicity?

What happens if we scale up and out Wallman's local, urban focussed arguments about openness and closure and map them onto more recent debates about Englishness and rural spaces?

It would be possible to suggest that we can see some of Battersea and some of Bow at work within the national story. There is certainly some openness within Englishness but this is uneven and tends to be time and context specific and subject to revisions and amnesias (see Hesse, 1992; Hall, 1992; Gilroy, 1987; 2004; Ware, 2007; Modood, 2007 for example). Alongside these unpredictable degrees of openness there tends to be an accompanying conditionality. What Wallman found in Battersea, in terms of an attachment to place enabling and facilitating routes of belonging, resonates at the national level and is particularly acute in relation to multiculture. I have argued elsewhere that inclusion in the nation is contingent on certain behaviours particularly of black minority and ethnic populations. The overwhelmingly hostile reaction to the publication of the *Future of Multi-Ethnic Britain* report (2000) is one example of this conditionality. The report was a substantial, policy orientated document produced by a multiethnically constituted Commission. The report in part called for a rethinking of the national story premised on a recognition of a colonial past and the need for a more inclusive account of what made up the contemporary British nation. The public and political reaction to the report centred very much on a defence of Britishness and Englishness which in part argued that Britain had always been an inclusive multicultural nation with nothing to feel guilty about and in part vilified the Commissioners themselves for being high achieving elites who were unfairly criticising the nation in which they'd become successful (McLaughlin and Neal, 2004; 2007; Fortier, 2007). This conditionality was commented on by Bhiku Parekh, the Chair of the Commission when he noted that,

> in politics, 'who says' is just as important as 'what' he or she says…Although the majority of our commissioners were white and of impeccable liberal credentials, the fact that there were so many high-profile black and Asian intellectuals gave the impression that the Commission and its report had a distinctly minority orientation. This imposed tangible and subtle limits on what the report should and should not say – limits which it could transgress, as indeed it did, only at its peril. (2001: 11)

In relation to rural spaces as I have argued previously (Neal and Agyeman, 2006: 117–9) the requirements of sameness, fitting in and conditionality are similarly dominant (see also Chapters 5 and 6). While there were different positions articulated by participants in regarding multiculturalism from some focus groups speaking of 'welcoming multiculture' and others articulating a sense that the countryside will inevitably become more multiethnic, there was a common thread to these in which belonging was contingent on 'fitting in' and being the same. It could be argued that there is always conditionality in discourses of localism and belonging. The 'background noise' of it is always loudest in relation to multiculture and notions of ethnic differences. So while Englishness is marked by and holds the potential for openness, cultural exchange and border crossings there are other exclusionary processes, racialised demands and anxieties which continually drag at these transformative possibilities.

It is these that connect to the defensive policing of the ways in which English ethnicity gets defined and this is reflected in the melancholic emphasis on the (selective) past in the endangered England argument. There are two key concerns. First, that these attempts to discuss anxieties over what Englishness is overwhelmingly happen through a discourse of loss. Second, that this 'loss discourse' is primordially and rurally framed. Take for example Paul Kingsnorth concern that Englishness has become 'de-cultured' – 'we can't sing our own folk songs or increasingly, cook our own national foods. We don't know what grows in our local area. We sneer at Morris dancers while we sip skinny lattes. We are cut off from who we are and where we have come from' (2007: 283). For Scruton too the emphasis is on loss, on damage being inflicted and the need for an identity to be protected,

> the old England for which our parents fought has been reduced to isolated pockets between motorways. The family farm which maintained the small scale and diversified production that was largely responsible for the shape and appearance of England is now on the verge of extinction […] The night sky is no

longer visible, but everywhere blanketed with a sickly orange glow, and England is becoming a no-man's land, an 'elsewhere', managed by executives who visit the outposts only fleetingly, staying in multinational hotels [...] and nature has responded, as is her habit, to culture. The species that helped to consecrate the English countryside – the firefly, the nightingale, the barn owl, the eagle, the roadside reptiles and hedgehogs, the newts of the ponds and skylarks of the meadows, even the 'darkling thrush' – are now rapidly disappearing. (2000: 254–5)

Following Barth, Sandra Wallman (1986: 230) argues that while the most common 'items' to be mobilised in terms of ethnic difference are 'language, history, territory, economic considerations' there is actually a limitless range of things that can be called upon to delineate an ethnic boundary. This is an important point in relation to Englishness, as these two passages illustrate, because it is rurally related nature and rurally related social practices that are particularly incorporated into the endangered/lost essence of the 'de-cultured' and 'elsewhere' ethnicity position. My suggestion as to why that might be is a simple one and follows the arguments made by Patrick Wright (1984). Rather strangely it is non-human things that are perhaps most able to resonate with notions of the primordial. The primordial works very effectively when it is filtered through ideas of soil, land, generations, nature and when it is connected to corporeal senses – to how and what we feel and a viscerally experienced ethnic identity. This process of ethnic assembling that draws on convergences between rural nature and the corporeal senses is one which I examine in more detail in Chapter 7. For now I want to consider an older account in which this process is very clearly captured. Patrick Wright quotes from Stanley Baldwin's well know description of Englishness being the sound of the 'hammer on the anvil in the country smithy', 'the sight of the plough team coming over the brow of a hill' the 'smell of woodsmoke coming up in an autumn evening'. According to Baldwin these are all things which 'strike down into the very depths of our nature and touch chords that go back to the beginning of time [...] these are the things that make England and I grieve for it that they are not the childish inheritance of the majority of the people to-day in our country' (cited in Wright, 1984: 82).

These extracts from Baldwin, which were written in 1926, are striking not only because they so closely resemble the worries of contemporary writers on Englishness such as Scruton, Kingsnorth and Askwith but because of the explicitly primordially framed connections between sense, self, ethnicity and nation that Baldwin's account sets up. As Wright argues in relation to Baldwin and other interwar writers – but it is equally applicable to more recent work of the texts I have been discussing – there is an 'interpretative stress on the senses, on the experience of meanings which are vitally incommunicable and indefinable' which contrasts sharply with how important and clear 'the sense of threat is to the definition of the deep nation' (ibid.: 83). In many ways this is why the changes that have taken place in the English countryside that were discussed in Chapters 1 and 2 have worked to galvanise and reshape the ways in which the rural spaces are so politically contested (Woods, 2005). It is impossible to view the form and turbulence of these politics of the rural as being somehow separable from notions of threat.

However, in arguing that rural nature gets to be mobilised, to use Barth's term, as a 'vessel' or container of ethnic meaning I want to stress that it lends Englishness what Wright describes as a 'vagueness'. It is, in some ways, this vagueness and the fleeting, ephemeral features of definitions of Englishness that are significant. In his discussion of the work of ruralist interwar writers Wright argues that even colours become crucial in this process, with green becoming 'the very ground of an England of the mind' and he goes on: 'the names – of villages, plants, landmarks, birds, stones and the accoutrements of rural life [...] which aren't used to describe a world so much as anxiously conjure one up' (1986: 109). Reading this in Wright's work chimed with the consistency with which references to rural nature things or objects were made by participants in the project. The following four extracts in many ways exemplify the emotionally rich, corporeal (the Dresham conversation in particular reflects this) but *imprecise* evocations of Englishness:

> Iris: This one [the group are looking at images of rural England] is ever so England.
>
> Researcher: Do you think so?
>
> Iris: Oh yes.
>
> Researcher: Tell me more about that. [lots of voices join in]
>
> Mary: Look at the dogs.
>
> Iris: That just says it all doesn't it?
>
> Susan: Is it the *light*?
>
> Iris: It's the *greenery* and the trees. (Farleigh WI. Emphasis added)

> Researcher: Is there anything that you would say is a particularly English about those views? [The focus group have been talking about their favourite views]
>
> Mark: The *green*. The green grass.
>
> James: Trees.
>
> Sally Anne: The trees yes. (Hetten YFC. Emphasis added)

> Barbara: I like an oak tree in a field I do.
>
> Researcher: Why oak trees in particular?

Barbara: *Because it's English.*

Joan: *It's solid.*

Barbara: Just like I say – it's English because I think fir trees are Scotland and oak trees are England.

Researcher: Is there a reason why oak trees mean that?

Nancy: It's probably historic. Probably because the oak trees of Britain built the ships.

Joan: You're talking about the [19]14–18 war, that's where they went. I remember my old neighbour, she used to grieve. She said 'they all went for buckets or for industry'. (Appleby WI. Emphasis added)

Elizabeth: I much prefer it [the English countryside] to Italy – Alan said 'shall we return to Italy' you know, I said 'no – I never liked it'.

Monica: It's like a tangible thing really. There is a *feel*, there is a *smell* isn't there? There's a smell. There's something when you stand there and it kind of envelops you.

Anne: *It sort of goes through the pores.*

Monica: It's just something you take in. Trees certainly.

Researcher: Yes tell me about trees.

Anne: We have lots of trees around here and we've got the Archley Estate which is beautiful and the drive down through the beech trees whatever the time of year. It's lovely in November in the mist and in the summer with the sun coming through the leaves […] I will never tire of it.

Researcher: Erm do you think that they're particularly English? You talked about beech trees or do you think of that as something you'd find elsewhere too?

Julie: Well you've got different trees abroad haven't you? […] Oaks and beech and ashes. Yes. All the English trees.

Anne: People talk about the cherry trees in Dresham. You know people who lived here years ago, they come back and they see the cherry blossom.

Julie: It's not quite Japan but it is lovely.

Anne: Wild cherries. It always sticks in people's memories somehow. (Dresham WI. Emphasis added)

In all four of these extracts what stands out are not only the ways in which light and colour and trees become the core pegs from which to hang Englishness but also the ways in which Englishness seems to flit ambivalently and uncertainly into, but then as quickly out of, these accounts. Even when the researcher deliberately prompts the participants to be more explicit as to what is English about the trees or the view the conversations are not able to define this, nor do the participants seem enthusiastic about doing this. For example while Julie asserts the relationship between certain trees and nation it is the cherry trees themselves that animate the group more. Similarly Nancy's response to the researcher's question in the Appleby focus group is a vague allusion to history which prompts memories of a neighbour's sadness over the cutting down of trees rather than prompting reflections on Englishness. Similarly Barbara's allocation of oak trees to England and fir trees to Scotland is not taken up more widely by the participants. There could of course be a number of factors reflected in this reticence so I do not want to overstate the suggestion. But nevertheless, what can be read in it is the ephemerality of the symbols that supposedly mark it out as an ethnic identity.

Conclusion

This chapter began by suggesting that notions of home are closely entwined with and embedded within notions of ethnicity. By beginning with this I intended to give a flavour of the argument that lies at the heart of this chapter that ethnicity involves and works through a range of human emotions. As Bondi et al. (2005: 7) note 'the close connections between boundary forming processes and emotions suggest that it may be productive to think of emotions as intrinsically relational [...] although highlighting the emotionally troubling hardships and injustices caused by inequalities and oppressions researchers have not generally considered the emotions that underpin them'. Ethnicity is invested with meanings and sense making processes because it works right at the intersection between the private interior worlds of individuals and the public exterior worlds of seemingly collective populations. This is why home works as a metaphor for ethnicity as it too works from the small scale of home/ethnic identity as the place of retreat and source of comfort and safety to homeland, which gets mobilised in much the same way as a place of retreat, comfort, safety and recognisable belonging.

The multiple meanings of home also reflect the ways in which ethnic identity and national identity continually slip between and fold into one another when the ethnicity is a majority and dominant identity as in the case of Englishness. I have argued in this chapter that it is important to stress that when ethnicity gets used as a way of ascribing those who can be marked out as culturally different and nation gets used to mark out conditional sameness, then it is important to approach Englishness is an ethnic category but with the important caveat that to analyse it in these terms is to focus on it as an assembled identity. Its very dominance means that defining the ways in which it is assembled is elusive because it is both multiply and mundanely located. As a dominant identity it works most consistently and in its most delineated boundary form in response to an idea of threat and so emerges most recognisable form as a defensive narrative of an imagined past and endangered present. The threat is multiply located as well as ever present, as the similarity of the worries of Stanley Baldwin and to the worries of Paul Kingsnorth some 80 years later evidence. Within this narrative the countryside has tended to be deployed as an endangered and essentialsed symbol of what Englishness is and this chapter has suggested that rural nature has been invested with the meanings and representations of English ethnicity.

While theories of ethnicity have tended to work with arguments which stress the social-cultural and instrumental basis of ethnic formations and have been rightly critical of primordial logics of ethnicity, casting English ethnicity through the optic of the rural and rural nature taps directly into 'naturalising' and ethnic stories which place value and meaning on profound, born and bred bonds to place and kinship. This works as a metanarrative of English ethnicity but in everyday contexts it translates into much less precise definitions. For example, the data that this chapter works with show that attachment to place is built and emergent from the interior worlds of individuals. In the conversations cited above participants did connect their everyday rural environments to definitions of what Englishness was but there was an uncertainty to these connections. They were expressed emotionally and often slipped from being about Englishness to more personalised meanings. Chapter 7 picks up on this duality in rural nature, working as a repository of ethnic boundary making but also working in shaping peoples' personal and private attachments to place and the things that surround them in the environments in which they live. In this way this chapter suggests that there is a further double bind to that which Wallman identified for ethnic identification.

On the one hand the very things that can be drawn into ethnic meaning making are open to multiple and diverse interpretations and so demonstrate the contingent and context specific basis of ethnicity. In this way it could be argued that ethnic identities are potentially open and unstable. For example in the Dresham focus group interview while some participants commented on the ethnic meaning of oak trees it was the cherry trees and the memories of them in blossom that were spoken of as tying residents to the village. In other words in this conversation the cherry trees worked at a more intense emotional register than the oak trees. On the other hand, however, the things that get drawn into such an ethnic identity process often carry intense emotional attachments which can contain and limit the inherent instability of ethnic identification. In other words the imprecise nature of allusions to Englishness is offset by their ability to work through the corporeal and visceral and emotional – it makes the things appear as more real that they are because the attachments are strongly and intensely felt. While I return to consider the possibilities and limits of this paradox (see Chapter 7) it is the ability of the category ethnicity to operate most effectively at the moment in which ontological securities and insecurities converge and collide that is significant. I noted earlier that it resembles community in this way and it is community that the next chapter returns to examine.

Chapter 5

Making Rurality: Practices of Community, Conviviality and Social Care[1]

Introduction

The argument that the concepts of rurality and community get continually folded into each other in idyllised and recursive ways has occupied most of the preceding chapters. Chapter 2 for example showed how this process continued to be an influential and tenacious one. Despite receiving critical and empirical attention and numerous commentators who have stressed the various ways in which the lived space of the countryside is a highly contested and heterogeneous site containing a range of socio-economic tensions, needs, socio-cultural exclusions and contradictions (Cloke and Little, 1997; Cloke, 2003; Sibley, 2003; Tyler, 2006; Neal and Agyeman, 2006 for example) community still overwhelmingly acts as the most effective short hand for describing rural social relations. I have suggested that this effectiveness stems from the imaginary and the 'fantasy' of community (Clarke, 2005) but what I want to explore in this chapter is the way that this fantasy becomes *enacted* so that community shifts from its abstract status into a material 'thing' that is created, sustained and experienced in and through everyday discourse and practices. This idea of an *experience* of community can be very explicitly heard in this Northumberland WI conversation:

> Elizabeth: You look after your neighbours.
>
> Sheila: You do.
>
> Several voices: Definitely.
>
> Joan: This is the best part of the whole thing. I mean when Ted and I were ill we couldn't have survived without our neighbours. They're always there for you.
>
> Daphne: I think it the community spirit.
>
> [...]
>
> Sheila: Daphne's husband works in – he's a butcher – he works in the butchers. And I mean he knew about everyone in the village. You know, you ask Mrs so-and-so how her pains are today or is her leg better. But this is it, people – and it's not nosiness – its just people/
>
> Joan: People care.

---

1   A version of this chapter first appeared in *Sociology* (2008).

Elizabeth: Yes, people care and if you're an old person and you go say into the butchers and Ned says 'how are you keeping today? Is your cold better' or something and maybe you haven't spoken to somebody for a few days that'll boost you. Then you'll think 'somebody cares'. It's just part of community life. (Dresham WI)

It is the idea of the social experience of community or the 'structures of community feeling' (to borrow heavily from Raymond Williams) which this extract appears to describe that lies at the heart of this chapter. In looking at how structures of 'community feeling' are created, affirmed and maintained in local rural environments, I suggest that extensive and intensive labour takes place and drives community making. However, it is important to recognise that, while I call it labour, this is very much a set of everyday efforts and practices that are socially and care orientated. Rural social organisations, such as the Women's Institutes and Young Farmers Clubs, which very much operate through and are embedded in, notions of conviviality and community, have taken up a particular place in processes of producing and sustaining the social and inclusive experience of community.

The chapter begins with a return to and development of some of the sociological tussles with the concept of community that concerned Chapter 2 and looks to debates on conviviality in urban settings to ask if these can connect with and help make sense of rural practices of community-making. The final parts of the chapter come back to the anxieties that the mobilisation of community tends to produce in academic analysis and worries about the relationship between rural social organisations and the governance of local social worlds. This raises a larger question for the chapter to address: what are the limitations of conviviality for producing inclusive rural communities?

Community and Making Community

As Chapter 2 noted any discussion of community usually always begins with the sociological health warning that it is a contested concept surrounded by debate. For example, Sergio Chavez, (2005: 30) with Hillery (1955) and Bell and Newby (1971) in mind, reminds us that sociologically community has 'some 94 definitions' and Brian Alleyne argues that 'community is so fundamental a concept encompassing as it does myriad ways of thinking and talking about human collectivities that it is quite unsurprisingly a term which is impossible to define with any precision' (2002: 608). This impossibility led sociologists like Margaret Stacey and Ray Pahl to publicly declare their frustration with the concept and urge a move away from it. However, this frustration has not led to a decline in social science's interest in community – this has continued to increase (see Chapter 2, Crown and Allen, 1994; Bauman, 2001; Amit and Rapport, 2002; Day, 2006; Young, 2007 for example). While it is not the intention of this chapter to map out in any extensive way the the contestations over community, it does commit itself to Alleyne's important suggestion that 'community always needs to be explained rather than be the explanation' (2002: 608).

Community has held an early and constant place in sociological inquiry. It was a focus for Emile Durkheim, Georg Simmel and particularly Ferdinand Tönnies (1963) whose association with the differences in social relations in rural and urban environments was developed in his famous *Gemeinschaft-Gesellschaft* cleavage. For Tönnies rurally organised, 'traditional' social relations could be defined through the concept of *Gemeinschaft*, which has been most commonly translated as community, and which was said to be defined through four core features – the biological, the geographical, the sociological and the psychological. In other words these can be defined as blood, place, everyday interaction and sensibility (Bell and Newby, 1971). Each of these is familiar in terms of their continuing populist and political associations with contemporary understandings of community. In Tönnies' critique of industrial capitalism it was the decline and loss of *Gemeinschaft* social relations which was a key concern and a measure of society's shifts into modernity. While 19th-century sociologists shared Tönnies' position on rural community social relations some, such as Simmel, viewed the city with more ambivalence seeing it as a site of 'objective culture', calculation, rationality and blasé attitudes on the one hand but also as a site of cultural and social possibilities and freedoms on the other (Ritzer, 2000: 165). However, the *Gemeinschaft* influenced concept of community – one tied to small scale, mutual interaction and to face to face reciprocal, interdependent social relations – has retained a particular folk and policy status. It has as Zygmunt Bauman (2002: 1) become a social relations ideal that works conceptually as 'the fireside by which we warm our hands'. Theoretically though the (empirically based) discontent that Ruth Glass, Margaret Stacey, Ray Pahl, Colin Bell and Howard Newby all articulated in relation to the concept has continued (see Chapter 2) to drive processes of re-thinking how to interpret community as a descriptor of social relations effectively.

This academic unease with a *Gemeinschaft* version of community has meant that social science led developments have seen community being moved towards the concept of boundaries (Barth, 1969); to a focus on its work as a symbolic cultural category (Cohen, 1985), and to an analysis of its ability to represent largely imagined human connections (Anderson, 1991). The maintenance or otherwise of the boundary, symbols and imagined connections and the ways in which these give rise to insider/outsider dualities have preoccupied critical thinking on community during the 1990s. For example Gupta and Ferguson (1997: 13) argue that 'community is…a categorical identity that is premised on various forms of exclusion and construction of otherness' and Weekes (2000, cited in Bauman 2001: 100) asserts that 'the strongest sense of community is in fact likely to come from those groups who find the premises of their collective existence threatened'.

Approaching community in this way has tended to recast what community means – locating it much more in a 'beyond geography', non-*Gemeinschaft* context. However, as Amit and Rapport (2002) have argued this mainly anthropological and sociological recasting has meant that studies of community have tended to be drawn towards the bigger dramas of tension, conflict, exclusion or the non-place based diasporic, transgressions and mutations of identities and identity boundaries. Consequently they argue that the social has been somewhat lost – there has been a 'mutual shift from an emphasis on actual social relations and groupings to symbolically demarcated categories of identity' (2002: 45).

In some ways, through an emphasis away from the contested 'hard edges' of community and boundaries and onto the structures of community feeling, what the project data provides a counter to the rather relentless hollowing out of community. This brings the social of community back in from the conceptual cold. While Cohen argues that 'community exists in the minds of its members and should not be confused with geographic or sociographic assertions of fact' (1985: 98) and concludes that 'people construct community symbolically, making it a resource and repository of meaning and a referent of their identity' (ibid.: 118) it seems important to suggest that the imagined community gives rise to a series of everyday labours to materialise the 'sense' of community. In other words there is a third space between imagining and feeling community that is filled with the routine caring and convivial practices for *making* community.

Thinking about the spaces in which conviviality and acts of kindness and care take place brought me to Nigel Thrift's (2005) efforts to filter cities through a politics of hope and kindness. Thrift suggests that the city-catastrophe coupling made by urban theorists such as Mike Davies (2006) obscures and marginalises the complexity and extent of the ever present and ever busy but easily overlooked and 'forgotten infrastructure of mundane activities' that routinely hold and bind cities together and which are 'not easily unravelled' (2005: 136). It is these everyday, ordinary practices which can provide the basis through which cities are able to recover, replace and recreate themselves. While not discounting urban misanthropy Thrift argues that cities also have to be thought of, designed and recognised as 'potential nests of kindness' (ibid.: 143). Viewing cities through such a lens reveals them as more than arenas of fear, mistrust and dislocation. Not only are cities spaces in which diverse and agonistic interactions are integral, and managed within them, but they are also affective sites in which small scale, 'lighter touch' urban politics 'generate trust and familiarity' and various 'mundane modes of social interaction foster binding common moods' (2005: 146). Thrift argues 'it is possible to suggest that the looser ties of friendship and conviviality...have the most to offer in keeping cities resilient and caring' (ibid.). Do these modes of compassionate sociality have as much relevancy to rural environments as to urban ones? In short, yes of course. And in many ways it could be argued that what Thrift is suggesting is extending rural modes of sociality onto/into urban environments. How different is Thrift's position here from that of Barbara Gill the former national Chairwoman of the Women's Institute when she commented that 'we must never underestimate the power of friendship and companionship. [The Women's Institute] need to show that, on the one hand we can influence decision makers; but on the other, it is a vehicle for women to meet, share friendships and enjoy each other's company' (*Guardian*, 3 December 2005).

As I have argued in the previous chapters rural social relations have always lent themselves to an easy association with care and kindness and mutuality rather than distrust and aggression and misanthropy. I have also argued that this does not mean that the latter are absent from rural environment (Cloke and Little, 1997; Sibley, 1997; 2003; Chakraborti and Garland, 2004). While it is striking that urban theory should (re)engage with the ideas of reciprocity and interdependency in many ways this underlines the impossibility of conceptualising social relations and practices in rural and urban spaces as distinct and different. Reflecting this Chapter 6 looks at how the freedoms and anonoymities that urban spaces appear to offer are as sought after and valued in rural spaces as evidenced in participants speaking of rural spaces as ones of being able to 'get away with loads', ones in which 'you can do what you want' and ones in which solitude and a lack of sociality are desired. Similarly even a very brief return to Chapter 2 shows how fantasies of mutually interacting, caring communities are as present in urban spaces as in rural ones. The contradictions of how we want to and do live in our spaces and places reflects, as Lauren Berlant (2004: 5) nicely puts it, 'the intimacy of daily life: people want to be overwhelmed and omnipotent, caring and aggressive, known and incognito' (cited in Thrift, 2005: 143). While there is then a rural–urban continuum in the desires of social relations and social practices what the chapter now examines is the idea that in rural environments the practices of conviviliaty and care are, via the narrative of community, very explicitly – and in the form of social leisure organisations, more or less formally – committed to.

Social Organisations, Conviviality and Communities of Practice

The value our participants placed on the local was particularly apparent. This was not only the background context in which the 'bigger themes' of friendships and social activities were established and organised – the idea of a local place and of having an attachment to it, was very much an integral part of and shaping these processes. While both the WIs and YFCs are organisations that have a national profile and campaign and lobby at a national level (see Chapter 1) – the WI particularly has a clear national agenda of concerns around a range of political issues from the closure of rural post offices through to GM crops for example – the project's focus group interviews revealed a lacuna between the national organisations' ambitions and 'political' activities and the motivations of the members of local Institutes and Clubs. Focus group respondents tended to speak of their membership of their organisations in relation to their local worlds not in terms of a wider policy agendas. Although there was pride expressed by WI members in relation to their national profile and campaigning associations this was often alluded to in a rather disconnected way as the constant slippage between first and third person in this excerpt shows,

> Marion: At a national basis we are sort of the ground level of various opinions which do get carried up. [murmurs of agreement]
>
> Audrey: Yes we do have some power.
>
> Marion: We've had a lot of clout over the years.
>
> Esther: Yes all sorts of things…
>
> Eleanor: There's quite a list of things they have fought for.
>
> Pam: If we put our backs into it we can make a difference/
>
> Esther: Yes that's right because there's such a big body of women when they get into London and they have got a lot of say. (Longhorsely WI)

Some WI conversations were much more explicitly hostile to the national activity of the organisation as the comments in this Northumberland focus group:

> Cindy: At our last meeting we were trying to find a delegate to go to Sheffield to go to the meeting up there. Now I didn't join our WI to do that sort of thing. I'm not interested in it. In fact I don't even like the group meetings but I do enjoy the local meetings because its my local friends and that's why I joined the WI and that's what I wanted to get out of it and to feel I've put into it as much as I get out of it but really only locally. I don't want the wider issues of it/ […]
>
> Val:/passing resolutions – I couldn't give a sausage but I like the people that come here. (Little Buckley WI)

As Val's comments suggest, the attachments and involvements of the project's participants to the WI tended to particularly focus on, and be framed by, their senses of locationality, neighbourliness and friendship as Val's comments evidence. The convergence of place and sociality worked across the generational categories. To an even greater extent than the WI focus group members the YFC focus group participants almost exclusively explained their various motivations for being in YFC as being part of a very local social world. For example, being part of YFCs provided respondents with opportunities to be able to make a different set of friends away from those at school, to date and meet sexual partners. YFCs clearly offered 'something to do' but membership of YFCs was also understood as a specific spatial practice in that it was defined as being a *country thing* to do. The idea of YFC membership being an expected country thing to do brings back Barbara's surprise at my non-YFC membership discussed in the previous chapter. Being a YFC member presents a way in which to fully 'be in'/belong to their particular *and* their imagined geographical place as the following conversations show:

Researcher: One thing we're interested in is what made you join the Young Farmers?

Susie: Because my friends were in it already. [Lots of yeses]

Ashley: Yeah I was going to say that. The social life and making new friends.

[...]

Susie: I wouldn't know half that the people we know would we if it wasn't for /I wouldn't have met you [Turns to Ashley]/

Ashley: That's right...

Helen: It's not just about farming, it's just about getting together. (Archley YFC)

Ann: Young Farmers is a huge thing around here though because I think we wouldn't socialise half as much as we do if we didn't have Young Farmers.

John: It's like a youth club for county folk. You know if there's nothing on, you can just go to the club and catch up with everyone else.

George: You have something to talk about as well.

Jade: It's a big group of people who've got something in common. (Calby and Dorning YFC)

Tina: I joined to meet a different group of people. [from college]

Geoff: Its going back to being in a rural community isn't it? Its part of being a rural community isn't it. (Swimbridge YFC)

Lesley: Its things like this YFC that bring you close together with other people.

Rachel: It provides you with something to do when you're stuck out here, sometimes you feel like you're stuck out here its like a way of getting together with other people/

Rebecca: It makes it much better when you're out here.

Lesley: Oh yeah, you appreciate it more, definitely.

Daniel: You meet so many people.

Rachel: The amount of people I've met [...] because you've got something in common haven't you?

Daniel: Yeah. Actually most couples I know have met through Young Farmers. [Lots of yeses]

Rachel: I think most of the parents here met through Young Farmers. Mine did. [Lots of agreement] And that's what keeps farming families together.

Rebecca: I'm sure my parents went to young Farmers with Amy's parents and Tony's parents.

Researcher: So they all know each other?

Lots of voices: Yeah. (Whitely Chapel YFC)

What emerges from each of these extracts is the importance that is simultaneously placed on locality, on sociality and on community. Young Farmers Clubs create social spaces in which young people perform specifically rural behaviours (see Geoff's comments in the Swimbridge focus group interview for example). It is in these social spaces that the production and maintenance of community occurs. There is something of Robert Putnam's 'bonding' social capital (2000) in the numerous comments made here as to Young Farmers Clubs bringing and then binding, people together ('Its a big group of people who have something in common', 'Young Farmers is a huge thing around here…we wouldn't socialise half as much as we do if we didn't have [it]'). There is also something of Tönnies' blood/kinship and the literal reproduction of community evident in the comments made by Rachel and Rebecca in the Whitely Chapel conversation as to the dating, sexual relationships and marriages that begin through Young Farmers Clubs ('that's what keeps farming families together'). Within all these accounts it is possible to identify a shared emphasis on sameness, recognition and commonality.

Like the YFC respondents the WI focus group participants also emphasised intimacy and friendship as being at the heart of their motivations to be part of a leisure organisation. Each of the following extracts offers a rich account of and glimpse into the importance of being in a local social network and the sense of belonging and mutuality that that is able to deliver:

Iris: There's great camaraderie and we have hell of a lot of laughs. [Laughter from the group]

Susan: Yes, yes it's wonderful […]

Mary: I didn't know anybody in the village and I thought '*Well if I don't go out and join the WI I shan't know anybody will I?*' I needed to meet everybody and find out who they all were and put them in the right houses! (Farleigh WI. Emphasis added)

Peggy: Friendship and the fellowship. [lots of yeses]

Betty: *Again the sense of belonging to something. [Lots of murmurs of agreement] Something that's much bigger than just 20 people sitting in the room.* (Burnham and Market Easton WI. Emphasis added)

Doreen: I think the social side is quite important.

Eva: Oh yes [...]

Doreen: It's a good basis for meeting people and having friendship, having a network...It's a very good support network. *We tend to look after each other if somebody's ill or something you don't just leave them to get on with it, the WI rallies round [lots of yeses].* (Dinburgh WI. Emphasis added)

Elizabeth: I was interested because I do think it's the only way people make friendships [...] *It's nothing to do with the needlework or anything else, it's the friendship. [Lots of murmurs of agreement and 'oh it is']*

Joyce: And when you want those friends they are there. And every woman in her life goes through a patch where she needs a friend. [...]

Susan: I thoroughly enjoy it and try and get other people to join and I think we have a lot of fun. We go on outings. It's a lovely afternoon where you go to meet your friends, have an interesting lecture and then a nice cup of tea and cake and then you go home again. [...]

Joyce: I just love WI and *it plays an enormous part* in my life. If I took WI in its entirety out of my life, well I'd just be reduced to dusting. [Lots of laughter] (Dresham WI. Emphasis added)

As in YFC accounts the WI focus group members constantly and movingly emphasised their commitment to and valuing of the idea of a very direct connection between their WI membership, friendships, and their senses of being cared for and of being part of a social community. Amit and Rapport (2002: 58–9) have argued that 'most of our experiences of communality arise out of the more or less limited interactions afforded by a variety of circumstantial associations, with our neighbours, the parents of children at our children's school, work colleagues, club members, team mates and more...but very often however satisfying and important these consociate relationships may be they remain contingent upon continued involvement in the association or activity in which they were formed.'

While it is important to acknowledge the fragility of the consociate relationship (or social network), the social relations evidenced in the YFCs and WIs focus group interviews appeared to represent more than *limited* moments of togetherness and connection. This suggestion is based on in three key observations: first, the extent of the emotional connections expressed; second, the dual emphasis that focus group members consistently placed on their belonging to a geographical place (their village/locality) and to an imagined rural community and third, the everyday efforts required in the ongoing construction and maintenance of structures of community feeling. These everyday efforts took considerable commitment. For Bauman one of the seductions of the notion of community is its ability to appear to 'tantalise' with its offer of a social space of security and mutuality – 'in a community we can count on each other's good will. If we stumble and fall, others will help us to stand on our feet again [...] our duty, purely and simply, is to help each other, and so our right, purely and simply, is to expect that the help we need will be forthcoming' (2001: 2). The structures of community feeling which were described by the focus group participants do more than chime with such tantalisations. They speak of the emotional experience of community. Nevertheless the fragility that Amit and Rapport note, means there is always an anxious space between the tantalisations of community and the desire for an almost tangible community. These anxieties about the absence of a sense of community are sublimated into numerous and various forms of community-making labours. It is these enactments of community at which rural social organisations like the WI and YFCs excel, as these accounts of the activities of Young Farmers Clubs and their social engagements with their wider local worlds show:

> We try and do some charity work throughout the year. We've done a couple of things already. We've presented a cheque to the local school and we went round delivering logs to the old people in Bellingham. (Bellingham YFC)

> I think our communities appreciate it don't they when we put on our Christmas Balls and bingo and things. (Archley YFC)

> It gets people from the rural community together. And now, with so many people like Laura and Jane coming in it gets towns people involved as well so its not just country, everybody is invited and is welcome and is joining in. (Great Histon YFC)

> I think it keeps traditions alive. Things Young Farmers have always done they still do. (Allerton YFC)

> Darren: It's the YFC that is trying to keep the community in the countryside. [Lots of yeses]

> Kirsty: For the farming population, or not necessarily farming but/

> Jon: /trying to keep the people together who have the same ideas.

> Chris: Yeah, the same interests. (Bellingham YFC)

What is particularly significant about these young people's conversations is the ways in which they bundle community-making practices which are directly about community responsibility and care – delivering logs for old people, presenting cheques to schools, organising balls for example – with social pleasure and conviviality. While the conviviality spoken of here appears to require sameness and conformity (as the Bellingham and Allerton conversations imply) there is a hint at the way in which convivial spaces can also bring in strangers and outsiders (see for example the Great Histon conversation). The WI focus group participants made similar intimate linkages between the sociality of community and notions of community responsibility. Again this looks, in many ways like a Putnamesque landscape of plentiful social capital, in which local organisations work as 'community glue'. Putnam argues that 'social capital can be [...] simultaneously a "private good" and a "public good". Some of the benefit from an investment in social capital goes to bystanders, while some of the benefit rebounds to the immediate interest of the people making the investments' (2000: 20). What is particularly striking are the levels of *energy* that participants in the study dedicated to this investment. The following descriptions evidence the individual and collective convergences involved in making and sustaining local structures of community:

> Pam: We've done lots of different things.
>
> Enid: We had a super day out last year. We went over Exmoor; we had a tour of Exmoor in various cars.
>
> Barbara: We made a Parish map.
>
> Pam: Yes, that was for the 75 year of the Devon federation.
>
> Wendy: And we made a millennium picture and we walked the Parish boundary, the whole 20 miles of it!
>
> Pam: Oh yes. [Lots of yeses]
>
> Enid: About 200 people came.
>
> Wendy: We organised the tea for the Queen's Jubilee.
>
> Enid: Oh and there's the village fete every year.
>
> Pam: Yes and we always have a float when we do the village carnival. (Little Buckley WI)

> We had the appeal for the prostate cancer unit and we've had our Open Gardens which is very, very popular and we put on teas which are very popular and every summer we have the traditional Farleigh Fair which dates back to when the Friendly Society was formed in 1869 and we also take part in the next village at Wighton Fair and last year it was their 750th fair and all our members, we had our own stall, we all dressed up in medieval costume and we sold our homemade cakes and other produce. So there is a lot going on in the village that we do. (Iris, Farleigh WI)

Iris' final comment not only speaks of the energies that go into organising these events but also alludes to the *extent* to which the WI in Farleigh occupies a central place in the village's practices of community. This idea of social organisations being particular sites of influence as well as activity within local social landscapes was evident in other interviews:

> Sylvia: *Well in our village it [the WI] actually brings the community together.*
>
> Jean: And it's a way of meeting because we've got no village shop and we've got/

Susie: /there's no pub.

Irene: *Anything that happens in this village is organised and sorted by the WI. Absolutely everything.*

Shirley: And it involves the men sometimes/

Irene: Oh yes the men get involved/

Sylvia: Like the millennium do and things like that, that's the WI/

Irene: That's right.

Jean: *It's the same group of people isn't it?*

Shirley: And we take our husbands out for a lunch at Christmas time.

Sylvia: And they come to the barn dance. (Rosing Dalling WI. Emphasis added)

Barbara: We have a WI hall and it's the only hall in the village.

Edna: Yes. *The WI is very important.*

Barbara: Very, very important.

Edna: Because we have various groups using our hall and without it there wouldn't be anywhere to meet/

Nancy: Without the WI there would be no hall. There was a time when the WI were responsible for about five evening classes a week/

Barbara: […] *I think we have the support of nearly everyone in the village because the – perhaps they don't want to come to the WI but they realise that the WI keeps the village together* and you have quite a few men who say 'you must go'. They know, the men, more than some women realise. (Edgham WI. Emphasis added)

Elizabeth: *The WI is so important to the village isn't it? [Lots of yeses].* The numbers have gone up recently/

Toni: And once a year we organise a ten kilometre race and get people from all over the county to come and run and every organisation in the village – on the back of that they can raise money for themselves. *So that is a real village.*

Ruby: And when I lost my husband the WI were a great support.

Elizabeth: And when any of us have been poorly we have all been very concerned about each other.

Ruby: It's a wonderful support isn't it?

[Lots of yeses]. (Dresham WI. Emphasis added)

What is being described in each of the above five accounts of everyday, convivial practices all map onto the sites identified in Thrift's lighter touch urban politics which were discussed earlier (2005: 145–7). We can see this fit in the descriptions of 'proto-political', small scale activities (raising money for local resources); in the creation of common moods (through ceremonial and celebration events) and in the narratives of friendship and kindness (care and support). In these accounts organisational skills, mutuality and commitment are each relational and spill over, and into, the other. These efforts directly contribute to a more tangible sense of community *and* they fuel the ongoing desire for 'community'.

However, what these accounts also evidence is the *political* capital of rural social organisations within the particular worlds to which they belong. This is very overtly described by Irene in the Rosing Dalling interview and is similarly present in the Edgham and Dresham interviews. In other words the WI does not appear, in these accounts, as *only* a convivial site of support and reciprocity – it also appears as an organisation which is influential in local processes of governance. One of the key social theorists associated with arguing that community can work as a site of social governance is Nikolas Rose (1999, 2000). For Rose, community is one of those routes through which the behaviour or conduct of populations is regulated, and where people learn to regulate themselves. Community becomes the *instrument* through which governments focus their strategies for controlling and regulating social conduct *and* for developing non-state based strategies for meeting the welfare and social needs of individuals, families and particular populations (Mooney and Neal, 2009). While some devolution of social well-being away from the centre and out towards the local and community is not troubling *per se* it is the difficulties presented by who and what is included/defined as being acceptable and an integral part of the local and of the community that are more troubling. Certainly there are senses of regulation, authority and a moral consensus as to what takes place locally that are evoked in the three WI conversations cited above. As Rose argues community works to bind 'individuals into shared moral norms and values; governing through the self steering forces of honour and shame, of propriety, obligation, trust, fidelity and commitment to others' (2000: 324). It is the ambiguities in the regulatory and/or reciprocal role of social leisure organisations and the potential limits of conviviality in rural social relations which I want to consider in this final section of the chapter.

Re/producing In/Ex-clusive Communities?

What is much in evidence from the project's data set and exemplified in the data cited is a narrative of community which appears to be unmarked by explicit symbolism, notions of a boundary, of insiders and outsiders, of external conflicts and struggle, of internal tension and the silencing of dissent. Amit and Rapport have argued that there are 'forms of community which are conceptualised first and foremost by reference to what is held in common by members rather than in terms of oppositional categories between insiders and outsiders. That is to say such consociation and the identities deriving from it are built through the shared experiences of particular associations and events. What matters most, therefore is what "we" have shared, not the boundary dividing "us" from "them"' (2002: 59–60). However, can the inclusive-social of community be divorced or clearly delineated from the exclusive-boundary of community? While the data provides a persuasive fit with the 'what we share' argument, at the same time it hints at some of the 'trouble' with community and community making practices. Some aspects of this 'trouble' are project specific but others more broadly relevant to community studies.

These troubles can be identified as *first*, the fragility of the data itself. Did the project elicit only very particular stories from its participants? I have argued previously that there was an element of Goffmanesque (1956) theatre – a management and public presentation of the 'best narrative' of rural and village life. This is not to argue that such best narratives do not exist but rather to suggest that the focus group interview tends to create a forum for collective conversations which reinforced consensus rather than allowing space for more diverse or contradictory truths to be expressed (Chapter 2, 3 and see also Neal and Walters, 2006). *Second*, conviviality may itself be fragile (Goffman, 1963; Laurier and Philo, 2005). The warmth of the conviviality expressed by the inclusive, non-other defined community may conceal more difficult emotions such as anxiety, boredom and loneliness. Certainly it was not uncommon for respondents to explain their membership of the organisations not only in terms of friendship and sociality but also as ways to avoid isolation and inactivity. Revisiting the data drawn on here shows how participants spoke of YFCs and WIs as 'something to do' and as providing a key focus for their lives 'when you're stuck out here' and as being the central way to have meaningful social connections – in particular it is perhaps Elizabeth's 'without the WI I'd be reduced to dusting' comment that stands out in this respect. In this way the narratives could be seen to reflect communities in which conviviality and sociality are technically and semi-formally *organised* rather than something 'naturally' or *organically* occurring. The notion of a manufactured structure of community feeling was something that troubled Alwyn Rees in 1930s Montgomeryshire. For Rees,

> the absence of real society is also manifested in the diversity of organisers, maintained by official and unofficial bodies [...] offering his own brand of social activity: an adult class [...] a Youth Club, a Young Farmers Club, a Women's Institute, a branch of the Farmers Union. It is profoundly significant that none of these activities is designed for the community as a whole [...] each local group established in this way is linked organisationally with others of the same type in other localities and with a central office [...] but there is nothing to tie the local units together on the spot or justify the one to the other [...] Thus does modern society try to instil new life in the countryside by commending to it its own specialisms. (1971: 170)

Rees' explicit concern was with the superficiality and disconnected nature of rural social organisations in local rural worlds but perhaps more significant is what he is more implicitly recognising i.e. how – as the participants' accounts of the community focussed work of both organisations reveal – extensive the influence of social organisations is within local rural worlds.

This is the *third* 'trouble'. In effect the WI and the YFC inhabit a powerful – if mundane – location in the local political landscape as they define, shape, reproduce and organise local ceremonies, events, occasions, activities and traditions. In a reflection of this role both organisations have quasi governmental structures – committees, presidents, treasurers – and processes – resolutions are tabled, conferences are attended and spoken at. However, neither the WIs or YFCs are appointed by, nor are they accountable to, the broader communities in which they take up (and claim) such a central place. Given this, it is significant that in the WI focus group interviews local people *outside* of the WI membership were identified as being supportive – whether it is (related) men as the Rosing Dalling conversation indicated or more generally as Barbara's comment implied in the Edgham WI focus group interview. WIs and YFCs could be seen as two social organisations which are very much part of what Woods and Goodwin (2003: 259) have described as the 'messiness and complexity of new structures of [rural] governance [which] raise questions concerning legitimacy, accountability and power'. The very mundanity of the organisations in many ways minimises (but does not destabilise) their power. It was not uncommon for respondents to laughingly reveal a form of a shame in terms of their connections to either organisation:

> That's another thing, you get teased at school if you go to Young Farmers [lots of yeses]. (Helen, Archley YFC)

> Townies think it's really sad though. I work and they say 'what are you doing tonight?' and I say 'Oh I'm going to a Young Farmers' disco' and they're like 'Oh my god!' and I'm like, 'It's not half as bad as it sounds'. (Chrissie, Calby and Dorning YFC)

> I went along under the theory 'oh lord I've been reduced to going to the WI' [Lots of laughter] […] whenever I'm going to something in the WI I always say it in hushed tones [more laughter]. (Val, Little Buckley WI)

> It wasn't until I moved to Devon that I was introduced to the WI by my neighbour here and I never thought I wanted to belong to WI [laughter from others]. My friends in Surrey still laugh about it. (Susan, Farleigh WI)

It is noteworthy that the triggers for being made to feel slightly ashamed all stem from outside worlds – it is school friends or urban based work colleagues in the YF accounts and it is the more recent arrivals in local areas in the WI accounts. However, if the *cultural* capital of both organisations is ambiguous this does not diminish the glow of their *social* capital.

It is in Susan's comments in the Farleigh WI focus group about being introduced to the WI by a neighbour that I want to address the *fourth* aspect of the 'trouble' with community i.e. the exclusivity of these social organisations. For all their being at the heart of community the extent to which they are open for outsiders to join and become members is not clear from the data. In the research accounts there appeared to be three ways in which membership was attained: first, through familial lineage and links – Young Farmers and Women's Institute members spoke of their parents and grandparents as well as older siblings being in either organisation. The idea of membership and belonging passed down through generations was relatively common and respondents often spoke quite proudly of such links. Second, through friendship networks and familiarity – this was particularly common amongst Young Farmers where they spoke of their friends already being in it and being taken along to meetings through this route. Third, through being invited – this was more a feature of the WIs where women were approached by an existing member and invited along to meetings.

While both the YFCs and WIs declared that anyone would be able to join by just arriving at a meeting – and some WIs said they advertised their meetings in the local newspapers and on local notice boards – in practice nobody that we spoke to in the project had joined either organisation in this way. This is not to argue that each of the three main entry routes for becoming part of the organisations are exclusive but that rather to emphasise their potential to be so. The local and social embeddedness of these organisations demands not only knowledge of them but also confidence on the part of anyone who did want to belong but lacked the 'maps' through which to find a way in.

Conclusion

This chapter has suggested that at a time when the concepts of conviviality, reciprocity and lighter touch politics is an emerging agenda in the social sciences (Gilroy, 2004; Thrift, 2005) then the everyday, small scale and mundane efforts of social organisations to construct local social relations through notions of community are worthy of attention. This follows Amit and Rapport's (2002) arguments that the *sociality* of community has become somewhat lost in processes of rethinking community as non-place based *boundary* on the one hand and as non-place based *imaginary* on the other. The empirical focus on everyday processes of creating and sustaining rural structures of community feeling has been an effort on my part to bring the social back in and 'fatten up' the concept of community because, as Barth himself noted, 'communities cannot be created simply through the act of imagining' (1994: 13 cited in Amit and Rapport, 2002: 20). However, while I have addressed the social of community as place-based and face-to-face I have also argued that localised and interdependent social relations contain a community imaginary and none more so than the 'rural community'. The chapter has emphasised the importance of two semi-formal social leisure organisations in this 'rural community' landscape. They operate at the moment of the coalescence of the real and the imagined and particularly aim, and are successfully able, to transform 'thin' social relations into the thicker relations of community and belonging. This occurs through an alchemic fusion in which mundane practices of conviviality and friendship are enmeshed with the desire for community and the everyday, small scale efforts to create tangible structures of community feeling.

At the same time, the focus group conversations appear to show how there are particular and specific processes of ordering and governance included within the sociality and friendship agenda. For example this raised questions as to the extent to which conviviality conceals more difficult emotions such as loneliness, anxiety and boredom and I argued that it is possible to re-read the data presented here and find those types of feelings mixed in with conviviality. Similarly there are issues about the legitimacy and accountability of unelected social organisations which identify and place themselves as at the heart of rural community and local practices of community making. Related to this is the argument that the sociality of the place-based local community that was much in evidence in the project's data does not so much spring from spontaneous, organic bonds but is produced and achieved through the remarkable energies of semi-formal leisure organisations. There is a technicism underlying and driving the (never finished) maintenance of structures of community feeling.

This focus on the micro processes of community-making does shed some empirical light on the contradictions, possibilities and the perils of using the concept of community in the analysis of contemporary, non-other defined, rural social relations.

Chapter 6

Competing Ruralities:
Convergent and Divergent Discourses
of English Countrysides[1]

Introduction

The previous chapters have each, at various points, all engaged with the way in which the idea of the English countryside as a picturesque place of sociality, safety and community has become so well-established that it has achieved status as *the* rural metanarrative and one that has occupied a particular and entrenched place in the broader national imaginary (see also Williams, 1979; Sibley, 1995; Bunce, 1994; 2003; Agyeman and Spooner, 1997; Bell, 1997; Matless, 1998; Neal, 2002; Cloke, 2004; Neal and Agyeman, 2006).

However, there are other narratives of rural spaces which, although they may not take up the same hegemonic position, do offer alternate readings of what the countryside might mean. Whilst far less entrenched, the rural has also been interpreted as a site of freedom and as space in which there is an absence of social intervention and regulation. Despite a body of academic work which has focussed on such interpretations of rurality (see Jones, 1997 and Valentine, 1997 and the geographies of childhood; Hetherington, 2000 and New Age Travellers for example) this is a less widely commented on, less acknowledged and less valorised cultural narrative of the rural. Its more marginal place reflects the importance of the rural as a space invested with notions of social order and Englishness in the national narrative. To have a counter or at least more multi-stranded narrative of rurality would unsettle this and would force an acknowledgement of the heterogeneity and difference which I have already argued characterise the English countryside. My own biography can be drawn on as an example of the notion of countrysides and of rural difference and I want to begin this chapter with some of this biography and the way in which it inflected the research process.

> Raised on a smallholding in the Pennines and then on a small dairy farm in West Wales, I had, until I was eighteen, a highly rural upbringing. As child this was filled with animals – including my pony – and days spent playing on the moors with my brothers or making dens in ruined farms. As an adolescent, living in the

---

1   A version of this chapter appeared in *GeoForum* (2007).

countryside became characterised by a dependency on either the rare bus service (last bus 9.30 pm) or parental goodwill (itself a rarity with a moody sixteen year old) and boredom. This teenage boredom was particularly spatialised as it centred on the desire for the city and for London, the 'ultimate city', in particular. I was not alone in the experiences of rural boredom and a dream of living in London of course. John Eyles thought of his childhood village as a 'place to be got out of rather than enjoyed' (1985: 12). He directly echoes my own metropolitan desires when he too describes his intensions to escape 'with total finality, the way many others do, by going to London' (ibid.: 13). Similarly, in her anthropological study of Little Midby, a village in Nottinghamshire, Anna Laerke (1998) describes how 'young people themselves told me of their longing to leave Little Midby behind, to travel and visit great cities, to move to "where things are happening". For everybody I listened to, boredom seemed to be the teenage condition par excellence'.

For most of my post-eighteen life I have lived in London and think of myself as deeply attached to it. And yet there is a pastoral draw. A rural embeddedness. The nature of the research project means that I reflect on the rural landscapes of my childhood and adolescence. My parents were from urban backgrounds but were rural idealists. They were part of a 1970s movement of young, often creative, dissidents who were to the political left and sought to escape capitalism and industrialism, suburbia and cities. They were drawn to rural remoteness, nature, alternative life styles and self-sufficiency. These painters, writers, potters, photographers and environmentalists bought abandoned cottages or farms – then plentiful and cheap – and taught themselves traditional rural skills and crafts and tried to live financially by them. I was raised as a vegetarian, without television, without an inside bathroom until I was thirteen and, until I was sixteen, without electricity. My house, a beautiful 18th-century farm that had long ago been left to house sheep and broken farm machinery, was bought and carefully restored by my parents and their friends and farmed by traditional non-mechanised methods. We were out of place and different to our farming neighbours – our relation to the land and our vegetarianism was equalled only in strangeness by our lack of television. This out of place-ness was quite apparent to me. Flagstone floors, range fires, gas lights, mullion windows, hay making by hand with a horse and cart may now make an unremarkable lead story in the country lifestyle magazine market but it all stood out horribly in the 1970s and 1980s and I tended to avoid bringing home friends from school. I can still recall my mix of longing – and disdain – for a farmhouse with wallpaper, carpets, a television and a farm with a John Deere tractor. My love of horses was in part my attempt to make a claim on a conventional, affluent, dominant rural identity. But only in part. My horse riding was of a non-conventional type – unconnected to riding school lessons and gymkhanas and more to do with freedom and the space of the moors that surrounded our farm. Reading Elspeth Probyn's (1993: 39) accounts of her and her mother's love of horses I recognised immediately their 'non-Pony Club' relationship with horses, of 'having to buy cheap horses saved from glue factories, a world in which riding was a rough passion...the desire for being at the very edge of control'.

When I was sixteen we moved to West Wales where I was more confident in my sense of rural belonging. In the early 1980s West Wales had become attractive to a significant number of English migrants and New Age Travellers seeking counter cultural lifestyles. While my family were still rather odd, there was a well-established 'alternative' population, living in benders, tepees and converted buses, for example, who began to make us look far less strange.

I have then an ambivalent rural identity. One in which I see myself as 'unincluded'. I don't belong to (though still desire?) a certain dominant version of rurality. However I am still clearly able to articulate a sense of belonging, despite my Londonness, to the countryside. So I am not excluded. I see my rural relation as one shaped by discontent and the desire to escape from it and the enjoyment and familiarity of the return to it. This ambivalence lingers over the fieldwork as the following example, documented in my field notes, evidences. At an early stage in the project's conception I visited Barbara, a key Women's Institute organiser in Hertfordshire and I wrote this account of our meeting in my fieldwork diary.

Barbara picks me up from the station and drives me to her large dairy farm that is a beautiful, semi-timbered Tudor farmhouse. It is the kind of farm I longed for as a child. It is July and sunny. We sit in her garden amongst the hollyhocks and I talk to Barbara about the project and other things. From where we sit I can see fields and hedgerows and trees. We are only about half-an-hour from North London but it would be hard to believe. I feel the need to mention immediately my own countryside connections. I notice and make a fuss of Barbara's dog, Sam, a lovely smooth-haired fox terrier and comment on what nice dogs they are. Barbara is impressed that I recognise Sam's breed. Fox terriers, highly popular in England in the 1930s, are relatively rare these days. I have a fox terrier myself and I tell Barbara this. My dog, with his associations of nation and history, becomes a symbol of my continuing rural authenticity (although his habitat is actually only North London parks). I am able to talk of dogs and farming and my villages in Yorkshire and Wales. There is a Goffmanesque (1959) sense of offering a performance of rurality and of a very particular rurality, the kind that I never actually had a convincing claim on when I lived in the countryside myself. However, this performance or 'impression management' (Goffman, 1959) is not a cynical exercise to ease research access but rather a means through which to build rapport, to say 'yes this is familiar to me, I know this/your world' and, after all, my own rural relation is part of my self. Nevertheless, it is a deliberate performance that draws upon a particular set of props and resources and is heavily inflected by class, Englishness and whiteness. It conceals, in what

Goffman describes in his dramaturgical approach as the 'back regions', the more dissident aspects of my rural upbringing.

> The performance is not without its potentially discrediting moments, for example when I have to admit that no, I was never a member of a Young Farmers Club and my Mum isn't in her local Women's Institute. These admissions are disruptions to my rural 'performance' and little indicators of my different rural identity. This different rural identity emerges again when Barbara invites me to stay for lunch. Lunch is a on a grand scale, the mythical farmhouse table piled high with food. Barbara's husband and one of her adult sons join us. What I had dreaded from the moment I accepted the invitation is of course there on the table; big plates of nicely laid-out hams and a large, meat pie! When she notices my meatless plate Barbara asks if I am vegetarian. When I concede this, she asks for how long. When I reveal that I have been brought up vegetarian and that my farming parents are themselves vegetarian there are again exclamations of surprise and doubt. Vegetarian farmers! How strange! I can't imagine how that works! Can they be real farmers?

I have started this chapter with this mix of positionality and fieldwork diary for two reasons. First, because of the influence of those scholars whose work has engaged with autobiography and geographic attachments and identity/ies and who have reflected on the relational nature of these to empirical and theoretical research and writing (see for example Williams, 1979; Eyles, 1985; Cloke, 1994). In presenting the intersections between the autobiographic self and the research encounter I am partially responding to Cloke's argument that, 'it is crucial to acknowledge some of the dilemmas in ethnography which arise from tensions between the ethnographer's self and the ethnographer's attempts to describe "other" subjects' (1994: 150) and I am partially responding to the task that John Eyles set himself. This was 'to make explicit my own sense of place...I want[ed] to expose those values and presuppositions that influence my interpretations of places' (1985: 8). The second reason is it illuminates the different experiences of rurality and different identities in rural communities. The tensions of the lunch experience in Barbara's kitchen, though small and rather comical, do, nevertheless, hint at the multiple interpretations and meanings that are attached to rural places. This chapter is concerned with the ways in which these multiple interpretations and meanings may diverge and converge. It focuses in particular on the discursive tensions between, on the one hand, idyllised, regulated rural spaces in which neighbours know each other and, on the other, 'freer' and non-regulated rural spaces where people can, as one participant put it, 'get away with loads'.

This chapter suggests that in scrutinising these tensions, there are strange moments of coherence and Foucault's concepts of panopticism (1979) and heterotopia (1986) are useful for unpacking the dynamics and ambivalences involved in the process of belonging to rural spaces. Using the concept of the panoptic stresses the place that the gaze occupies both in the rural community metanarrative and in the regulatory everyday rural practices that seek to maintain orderly social relations. The second section of the chapter focuses on the linkages between rurality and notions of freedom. Arguing that a particular space can simultaneously contain within it a range of 'extra' spaces, the chapter uses the idea of the heterotopic rural, i.e. a multiple space in which various notions of freedom are either practiced or desired. Although the focus group interviews do reveal some generational differences in their interpretations of rural spaces these differences were not always fixed predictable ways nor always easily delineated.

The Rural as a Panoptic Site: Regulated (and Regulating) Rural Space

It was noted earlier how the notion of a pastoral England is one that lies at the heart of particular imaginings of nation and is predicated partly on 'natural' picturesque landscapes and partly on 'social' community villagescapes. As Bell comments 'in Britain the rural idyll is a settled landscape mapping out a *social order* across a picturesque terrain – especially in its construction as "village England"' (1997: 95. Emphasis added). As Chapters 1 and 2 discussed, much of the appeal of the rural in contemporary England, as a place of residence and a place to visit recreationally, exists through an entangled and inverse relation to the urban. Anxieties about national identity and urban environments have restressed the rural as not only attractive as a 'natural' landscape, but also attractive in terms of its social landscape. This chapter initially extends some of the concerns of Chapter 5 and continues to think through the appeal of small-scale, neighbourly and intact communities but with an emphasis on their orderliness as well as the senses of social care they offer. The following excerpts from both Women's Institutes and Young Farmers' Clubs focus group interviews demonstrate some of this composite mix:

> Jan: I think you know more people in the country because you can live in the town and not know the person who lives across from you.
>
> Paula: I know everybody in Attlebury and there's always somebody there who'd help you out [lots of yeses] whereas it was never like that in/
>
> Jean: If you stand outside the door and yell for an electrician about ten would appear. [lots of laughter]
>
> Paula: I certainly do feel that I belong here even though we lived for a lot longer in London. (Attlebury WI, Hertfordshire)

> Annette: Brinham…was like one big happy family, everybody knew everybody and every door was open to everybody.
>
> Julia: Yes that's true and you knew everything about everybody.
>
> Annette: […] I left Brinham for five years but I couldn't get back quick enough.

Researcher: Why?

Annette: Because it wasn't the same. I was used to that big family being there. (Brinham WI, Northumberland)

Lee: I've lived on a farm in White Ford all my life. I've never wanted to live in Highton [the nearest large town in the area]. I found that there's like a better community spirit around here. The people you've grown up with and went to school with and stuff and you know their parents and their families and everything and there's always stuff to do everyday. People get together and you know them all as well.

Researcher: And that's important?

Lee: Yeah.

Researcher: Do you think you'd miss that if you/

Lee: Yeah. If you moved to a town or something you'd just shout at the people next door and stuff. (White Ford YFC, Northumberland)

The social order and the social care that is being described here has been part of the drivers of the rural repopulation of the English countryside (Halliday and Coombes, 1995; Halfacree, 1997; *State of the Countryside Report*, 2004). As Chapters 2 and 5 suggested the desire and pursuit of a rural idyll, centred on the reassuring idea of community, has become increasingly pronounced at the end of the 20th century and beginning of the 21st century. What the community making practices described in Chapter 5 tended to share was a heavy reliance on the notion of 'neighbour knowledge' and the importance of the informal and formal processes of watching and surveillance and it was the respondents' emphasis on the role and labour of the gaze as a core basis of community that seemed to make a number of connections to Foucault's notion of panoptic surveillance.

Arising out of his work on power, one of the best-known of Foucault's concepts has been that of the panoptic. Foucault theorised power as circulatory and multidirectional rather than linear, top down and (only) institutionally-based – 'it is something which only functions in the form of a chain' and is "net-like"' (1980: 98). Within this chain, individuals are 'the vehicles of power and not its point of application' (1980: 98). Multiple, non-linear power relations involve persuasion and self-regulation and the internalisation of what are defined as appropriate forms of behaviour or sets of practices. Thus individuals are not necessarily continually externally coerced, but rather restrain and limit themselves. Part of this internalisation process depends on the persuasiveness of particular regimes of truth. It also involves the continual possibility of behaviours and practices being observed, of an imagined monitoring of behaviours and practices.

Foucault drew on Jeremy Bentham's architectural design for a prison in which a central watch tower is surrounded by a building made up of individual cells. From the watch tower each cell and its inhabitant is perfectly and completely visible. Each cell's inhabitant is constantly aware of the watch tower and the possibility of being seen. This possibility is crucial as the inhabitant of each cell does not know if and when s/he is being observed from the tower. The uncertainty of the presence of the surveying gaze – of what Foucault called 'permanent visibility' (1977: 201) – produces conforming rather than transgressive behaviours in the inhabitant of the partitioned space. Those in the watch tower are not seen but they see all. Foucault saw Bentham's Panopticon extending in material and abstract forms to a number of social institutions – the prison of course, but also hospitals, schools, factories, universities and the family – and to the self-limiting/disciplining behaviours of citizens as power is exercised *through* them (Norris and Armstrong, 1999: 5). Post Foucauldians have argued that increasing surveillance techniques and capabilities such as CCTV and data collection and management can be analysed through the lens of the panopticon in which two panoptic stories, of those who gaze and those who are gazed upon, that can be identified (see Norris and Armstrong, 1999; Simon, 2005: 4 for example).

However, in viewing the rural community through the idea of a panoptic story this dyad becomes less distinct and the direction of the gaze more complexly constituted. For example the respondents in the focus group interviews, particularly those from the Women's Institute groups, routinely spoke of simultaneous processes of watching *over* their neighbours, of actively valuing being watched over and of engaging in processes of watching *out* for those figures they did not recognise. One of the most obvious forms that this nexus of the surveying gaze takes is in the development of Neighbourhood Watch schemes which, as Yarwood and Edwards (1995: 447) note, have 'flourished' in rural areas – 'roadside signs indicating their operation are a familiar sight in many rural settlements'. It is the intersections of the panoptic gaze and the slippage into concepts of community that Sara Ahmed refers to in her discussion of Neighbourhood Watch, 'the "good citizen" is one who watches (out for) suspicious persons and strangers and who in that very act, becomes aligned with, not only the police (and hence the Law) but with the very imagined community itself whose boundaries are protected *in the very labour of his look*' (2000: 30. Original emphasis).

It is the desired, inter-acting and explicitly acknowledged everyday process of *seeing* and *being* seen that is particularly apparent in this part of one of the Women's Institute focus group conversations:

Ira: They [insurance companies] wouldn't insure us unless we'd fitted burglar alarms and I said, 'Look my neighbour's not far away. *She knows everything that I do.* She'll see burglars. I don't want an alarm...' But the insurance companies don't know that; don't take it into account at all.

Janet: We've got two [alarms] but only because we were used to it.

Patricia: There's another reason for feeling safe here. It's because I know my neighbour. And my neighbour has always looked after me. *Any strangers around, they do get questioned.*

[Voices murmur yes in agreement]

Susan: *Everybody knows everybody.*

Patricia: And it's lovely because if something happens I know I can walk down the lane and there's someone there to talk to.

[Murmurs of agreement] (ChadworthWI. Emphasis added)

Knowing and caring for each other's neighbours involves and is contingent upon a process being surveilled. Community is 'made' and practiced through enacted forms of surveillance – Ira's neighbour would 'see' any suspicious activity and Ira's neighbour 'knows everything' that Ira does. Ira's confidence in this is such that she tries to reject a burglar alarm. It is this 'benevolent' aspect of the panoptic gaze that in part makes the participants talking here feel safe and secure as Patricia's comments demonstrate. The other part of their security builds on the regulatory panoptic gaze which is articulated through the assumption that anyone who isn't recognised or familiar will not only have their presence in the village noted, but will be actively investigated and 'questioned'. For this focus group it is the sense of security produced by such practices which are particularly commented upon:

Susan: It's wonderful. It's like a breath of fresh air and to me its how life was a good 30 years ago. That's what I like. Everybody feels safe. I just feel so safe here.

[…]

Ira: And if you promise not to tell the insurance company – but I forget to lock my doors!

Susan: Yes and leave your windows open and that sort of thing. I mean we're so conditioned to locking everything but you don't have to.

Reenie: We haven't got a key to our back door.

Janet: It's one of the reasons we moved here.

However, as Cochrane and Talbot (2008) suggest there is an indivisible quality to the relationship between security and insecurity and within a number of the Women's Institute focus group conversations in particular this was often evident. Yarwood and Gardner (2000: 405) have argued, although countryside areas are low crime areas, the fear of crime (particularly against property) has a significant presence. This fear connects directly into everyday practices. For example, in this

North Devon WI group there are accounts of a diminishing sense of safety which underline the necessity for both informal and formal surveillance:

> Margaret: I mean we've got a Neighbourhood Watch Scheme *but apart from that I think people would look out for each other in any case.* I mean we don't perhaps have to lock our doors. We probably do nowadays, but it's freer. It's easier.

> Anne: Years ago my aunt came to stay and I had a tiny window and I left it undone and she said 'Aren't you going to shut your window if you're going out?' and I said 'No, nothing will happen.' But nowadays you wouldn't. [Murmurs of agreement] My front door is always locked.

> Mary: Yes 50 years ago/

> Anne: And you are aware. If I see a strange car and it shouldn't be there I try and take the number. [Lots of yeses from the group] I belong to Horse Watch. I mean things get pinched. We had sheep [these were not Anne's sheep] down the road the other day in the field and I am sure there's one missing. My husband counted them and said 'I can't make it the right number' and we went down and we counted them and we walked all round and there were no dead sheep and they couldn't get out so somebody must have pinched the sheep. *You are wary.* (Rosingdean WI)

What is striking in this conversation is the extent of the labour involved in the processes of watching and being watchful in the village. The vocalised consent from the group more widely implies the extent to which such practices are common and shared and considered necessary and unremarkable. In this account strangers are challenged, unknown cars are identified, and the numbers of animals in nearby fields are known and monitored. What the members of these focus groups describe is a micro world in which constant and semi formalised (Neighbourhood and Horse Watch) processes of observation and regulation do, and need to, take place. The sense of security and reassurance identified by these participants is contingent on a collective and explicit awareness that the gaze occurs.

Within this context there is, as Ahmed (2000: 28) describes, 'a constant shift between an emphasis on a caring community and a safe community: a safe community moreover is one in which you feel safe as your property is being "watched" by your neighbours. A link is established here between safety (in which safety is associated with property), a discourse on good neighbourliness (looking out for each other) and the production of community as a purified space ("a new community spirit").' The panoptic gaze makes those who are included within the boundaries of the community feel secure and subscribe to the same set of behaviours – i.e. the social practises watching and engaging in knowing. It is important to acknowledge the value that is put upon the observation and monitoring by those who see and those being seen. The experience of community inclusion and belonging are enhanced by the perception of being watched over and of watching. Yet, if the rural as the space of community and safety represents a particularly panoptic site, what potentially and simultaneously unsettles this is the ability of the same rural spaces, and, at times, the *same* rural voices, to offer another story. While the articulations of the surveillance-neighbourliness relation were overwhelmingly located within the Women's Institutes groups, the themes of community and neighbourliness were articulated by both types of focus groups as were seemingly paradoxical narratives which valued the absence of (certain types of) regulation of rural spaces. It is these that are now considered.

The Rural as a Heterotopic Site: Unregulated Rural Spaces

As I suggested earlier although the narrative of the rural as a place of social harmony, community and neighbourliness is one that is particularly dominant, rural spaces have, at the same time, an appeal to, and association with, notions of social and cultural freedom and isolation from the tentacles of socio-legal governance (Sibley, 1997; Hetherington, 2000). John Urry captures some of this when he explains that, 'the countryside is thought to embody some or all of the following features: *a lack of planning and regimentation*, a vernacular quaint architecture, winding lanes and a generally labyrinthine road system and the virtues of tradition and *the lack of social intervention*' (2002: 88. Emphasis added). The association of rural spaces with freedom and the *absence* of a regulating gaze is not confined to the countryside. It is the quasi-rural spaces – parks, commons, Victorian cemeteries – of cities and urban areas that have drawn and been associated with various forms of unregulated, deviant and/or criminalised behaviours (see Jones and Cloke, 2003 on anti-social behaviours in city woodlands for example). There is something about the absence of people and the spaces of nature themselves which engender senses of freedom. That rural spaces or spaces of nature can produce this response evidences the ways in which the rural escape being totally confined to one singular meaning. This was reflected in many of the focus group conversations as more multiple and contradictory versions of participants' accounts of their attachments to rurality emerged. Participants revealed their engagement in routine sets of everyday practices which were at odds with the regulated social order version of rural spaces discussed above.

Lefebvre's concept of 'lived space' or 'representational space' and Foucault's concept of heterotopia both offer a lens for viewing the tensions in narratives as to what the English rural 'is'. For Lefebvre 'lived space' – the third element of his simultaneously occurring triad of perceived, conceived and representational space – is the space of 'possibilities and perils' (Soja, 1996: 68). Lived space is the space that is navigated and struggled over and within; it is the space in which acts of resistance, transgression and change occur (Lefebvre, 1991; Soja, 1996 and in relation to the rural see Neal and Agyeman, 2006). Hetherington (1997: 70) argues there is a certain romanticism in Lefebvre's 'lived space' because of its focus on social struggle and transgression. Hetherington works with Foucault's notion of heterotopia which he suggests can be understood as 'spaces of alternate ordering'. For Foucault, heterotopia was definable as 'the curious property of being in relation with all other sites but in such a way as to suspect, neutralise or invert the set of relations that they happen to designate, mirror or reflect…[heterotopia] juxtaposes in a single real space several spaces, several sites that are themselves incompatible' (1986: 24–5). The idea of a plurality of sites in which other forms of ordering take place but are contained within a particular space (such as the rural) is one that is relevant for understanding the project findings in that it allows for contradictory and different interpretations of spaces to simultaneously occur. Heterotopia is particularly appropriate because the freedom, non-regulatory rural discourse is not necessarily a counter-hegemonic one in the tradition of social resistance. Given that the project focussed on the rurally included and on processes of inclusion, the accounts which valued non-regulation constitute *alternate*, rather than *incompatible*, articulations of the regulated rural narrative.

In the focus group discussions the unregulated rural narrative emerged most often around the idea of being free. While there was diversity in the ways in which freedom featured in focus group accounts, the notion was most commonly linked – and inter-linked – in three key ways: in the articulations of emotional attachments to local rural spaces (see Chapters 4 and 7); in the descriptions of unregulated and anti-orderly rural practices; and in assertions of the autonomy of rural spaces from urban-associated socio-legal governance. The chapter now looks at each of these.

First, the emotional expression of the desire to 'be free' was framed by participants through a spatialised unaccountability. By this I mean focus group conversations would emphasise the ways in which they valued rural spaces because they appeared to offer the opportunity of being able to go where you wanted and of being the only one in 'people-free' environments. This extract from a Northumberland Young Farmers' focus group discussion works as a particularly effectively example of the 'being free' relationship to rural space:

> Researcher: Is there anything else you really appreciate [about living in the country]?
>
> Karen: You've got plenty of space to yourself.
>
> Researcher: Yes, tell me a bit more about that.
>
> Karen: You can just get on your bike and go – you've got places to go whereas in a town you'd be constricted to/
>
> Andrea: If you're in a bad mood you can just go away for hours and can just come back when you feel like it and no one will be able to find you. You can just get on a horse and bugger off and come back three hours later.
>
> Researcher: What is it about being up there that really appeals to you?

Andrea: It's just that there's no one else but me – and the horse.

Hettie: I think I'm the same as Andrea. [I] just like being independent. You can do what you want and you can just get away and think about stuff. (Barnley YFC)

What are revealed in this account are the opportunities afforded by rural space – not only to 'just get away from it all' but more significantly get away from the authoritative gaze. This is evidenced in Tracey's comment of no-one being able to find her and Hettie's echo of this in her comment about independence and doing what she wants. Given the age of the respondents in this interview group, it is easy to read the rural in these articulations, as offering a space away from *adult* order. There is of course a significant commentary on notions of regulation and non-regulation in the relationship between children and the countryside (Valentine, 1997; Jones, 1997; Holloway and Valentine, 2000). For example, Jones has suggested in his discussion of the rural geographies of childhood, that many accounts of growing up in rural areas contain 'strains of anti-order' in which certain rural spaces – derelict or abandoned farm buildings or 'untidy or forgotten about corners are more conducive for children because "normal" adult ordering has not taken place' (1997: 173). In their study of teenagers in Northern Scotland, Glendinning et al. (2003: 151) found feelings of 'autonomy' were 'associated with well-being in youth'. Reflecting these findings, the young people speaking in the Barnley Young Farmers focus group provide an account of a desire for escape from adult ordering and, at the same time, reveal a particular sense of *confidence* and *agency* in being able to move through familiar landscapes (e.g. in being able to 'just get on a horse and bugger off for three hours'). It is this combination that is also present in this contribution made later in the same focus group interview,

Martin: I would just say that I like it on the fell, on my motorbike and that me and my mates, my best mates, have got quad bikes as well so I just like going out on the fell and just being able to be…just being able to go out on the fell that's what I like about it. [the countryside]

Researcher: So is this your land or do you go on other peoples' land?

Martin: No I don't feel the need to go on anyone else's land because we've got, we've got loads of it.

The appeal of 'feeling free' is perhaps not a surprising rural value when it is being vocalised by young people. However, it was by no means solely confined to Young Farmers Club focus group members. It is possible to hear some of this same confidence about being part of a material *and* abstract place in Ruth's description of her enjoyment of the Hertfordshire countryside:

Ruth: I think I'm like everyone else I just like the view. I like to feel like/ like when I'm out on my bike, and I bike a lot, and you can cycle round and you can think, 'Yes this is my country and I'm free'. I like the sense of freedom and not being closed in and going out and enjoying it.

Researcher: And is there something about the landscape for you that is particularly English, when you're cycling around?

Ruth: Just the freedom, its just the freedom you feel, the wind, y'know even if it's wet, it's just great because you don't feel closed in, you just take the fresh air. (Appleby WI)

The connectivities that Ruth makes here between the natural world (the wind, the wet, air), with feeling free ('not closed in') and with a sense of nation and identity ('yes this is my country') very much echo some of the thinking presented in Chapter 4 and which is returned to in Chapter 7. However, it is Ruth's repeated use of the term 'freedom' and her re-emphasised comments on not feeling 'closed in' that are particularly significant in terms of there being a more widely shared sentiment in the focus groups and in terms of their relation to ideas of neighbourliness and community. Despite the extent to which community was valorised by the focus group interviewees there was a significant number of the same people who spoke of the importance they placed on an *absence* of social responsibility and relationships:

Winifred: This is why I like the country because of the trees and the views and the lambs in the field and all those sort of things.

Shelia: And the *lack of people/*

Winifred: Well that's right/

Shelia: You can go for a walk and *you're on your own/*

Wynn: Well that's right. *I mean you can go out and not see anybody at all.* (Emphasis added)

The desire for a lack of people emerged a number of times. This conversation below is from the same Women's Institute focus group that was cited earlier talking about calling for an electrician and ten appearing to help.

Paula: It is a very, it's a, people don't know this bit of Hertfordshire, going that way you're in Stevenage and it gets very built up. This way there is nothing for a long, long way and you can go cycling and *you don't have to go through any villages or anything really.* You can do a good 20 mile circuit and not hit any –

Researcher: So for you it's a sense of being away from/

Paula: Yes.

Researcher: From people?

Paula: Yes definitely.

Researcher: Do you have any sense of why that's important to you?

Paula: I suppose because we're quite quiet people. Not gregarious. [Lots of laughter as the others don't see her this way] But we're not honestly; I mean *if I could shut myself away I would feel really quite happy.* You say [turns to Jean] about working in the garden all by yourself. It's lovely. It's fine.

Jean: Yes. And the pheasants come in.

Paula: *I think I could very easily become a recluse...*It's lovely just to be able to have a whole, you can go out on your bike and have a whole day, *not meeting anybody*, not having to make conversation. It's lovely. [Laughter from group] It's nice doing it but its nice having not to have to do it. (Attlebury W.I. Emphasis added)

In all three of these conversations what is particularly notable are the apparent ambivalences and tensions being revealed between the earlier expressed attachments to the sociality of community and the appeal of an absence of sociality and of (sometimes) living, if not outside, but at least at a distance from, community.

The second strand in the rural spaces as spaces of freedom is much more about the exterior world. The absence of people that emerged above and the imagined (and real) remoteness of some rural areas contributed to a sense of there being a limited reach to the socio-legal gaze of the state. It is this idea of limited, or thin, formal governance that regularly emerged in focus group interviews. For some participants it was the feeling that in rural spaces they could do as they wanted. Accounts of a sense of an absent socio-legal gaze were a remarkably strong feature in many of the focus group conversations, especially in the remoter rural spaces of North Devon and Northumberland and it was overwhelmingly articulated by the Young Farmers' Club interviewees. A dissident notion of *anti-order* was expressed not only in relation to their own behaviours and accounts of particular events, but also in their opposition to attempts at regulation and socio-legal intervention.

It is the apparent juxtaposition of the social orderliness of the rural and the valuing of freedom from socio-legal norms that demonstrates the liminal and contested interpretations made on rural spaces. This point has been made by other rural scholars who have for example emphasised the distinction between 'crime' which is culturally acceptable within rural imaginations – smuggling, poaching and more recently (in the post-fox hunting legislation) hunting for example – and 'crime' which is not – raves and trespass for example (Sibley, 1995; Yarwood and Gardner, 2000: 404). In this context, my concern is to also evidence the *contained* nature of these transgressive readings of rural spaces – they are incongruous with the rural being conceived of as *the* site of social order but at the same time they do not disrupt rural social order *per se*. I would suggest that the kinds of dissident discourses and the everyday practices associated with this evidence *other* but not *counter* modes of rural ordering.

The types of unregulated or anti-orderly behaviours most commonly revealed, with a mixture of bravado and caution, by younger respondents were under-age driving and to a lesser extent, under-age drinking and ownership of guns:

> Annie: You've got much more of your own space and can do whatever you want really without people being in your face all the time [...]
>
> Lorna: [It's] just the freedom of being where you want to be and doing things that you can't do in the town.
>
> Researcher: Like?
>
> Lorna: Drive. Like I have a car and I can drive in the fields and I couldn't do that in Highton.
>
> Sean: Can I just say she's fourteen!
>
> [Lots of laughter]
>
> Researcher: Is there anything else?
>
> Pippa: Yeah, you can get away with loads because there's no one there.
>
> Sean: Shooting.
>
> Researcher: OK.
>
> Annie: It's mostly illegal like. Everyone drives.
>
> Mark: Yeah, I've got a car.
>
> Annie: And quads and motorbikes and tractors.
>
> Researcher: You don't have to answer this but do you mean when you say you drive you just drive on the farm or do you actually drive?
>
> Pippa: Oh not around. Just on private land.
>
> [Some laughter]
>
> Voices: Well/ They're country roads. You don't get many people on/ The back roads. It's just a little stretch it's not/. (Green Leigh YFC)

In another Northumberland Young Farmers' focus group an almost identical conversation took place:

> Jenny: It's very much a freedom thing isn't it? Living in the country, you've got no hassle, I mean you don't have the police cars roaming about do you? Nobody bothers you. You can just go where you want and when you want.
>
> Nick: Yeah. If a police car comes around here you look up! [Lots of laughter in the group]
>
> [...]

Dan: If you're going to learn to drive you're going to come out here aren't you? Its quiet roads/

[...]

Jenny: I learnt when I was out there when I was about fifteen.

Laurel: Yeah.

Nick: As soon as I could touch the pedal I was roughly doing it. Like by seven or so. It's an extra hand doing jobs on the farm, that's what it is/

[...]

Simon: Yeah, it's second nature to you by the time you're fourteen, fifteen. Come seventeen it's just a formality doing a test. (Hetten YFC)

Again what is remarkable, besides the symmetry of these conversations, is the emphasis that is placed by these respondents on the absence of the police and a wider socio-legal gaze ('you've got no hassle'). The presence of a police car is spoken of as something strange and unfamiliar in an environment in which the perception and confidence of being able to do what you want and go where you want ('nobody bothers you') is very ordinary. This is again present in these comments,

Lee: You can get away with a lot more things out here than you, well/

Robert: Yes there's less squealers around.

Sue: Tell me more about that.

Robert: No please, I don't want to go into that!

[Laughter in the group] (Edge Ford YFC)

In accounts of unregulated behaviours the regulatory figures that are present are locally and culturally embedded. Of course this is not to imply that there are no concerns about such behaviours in rural spaces. Yarwood and Gardner (2000: 407) detail respondents from their research expressing concerns about young people 'hanging around' in village squares, joy riding and underage drinking. However, in the narratives of illegal behaviours that were told in the interviews adults appear to either encourage, or at least not explicitly, oppose them. This accommodating or 'turning a blind eye' behaviour of adults disrupts the notions of the countryside as *the* safe place to grow up that Valentine (1997) documents. What it also does is demonstrate the spatially specific cultural underpinnings as to what constitutes risk and danger for children and adolescents. For example Rebecca, a member of a Northumberland Young Farmers' focus group interview, recounts how 'most of us have been driving before we were ten at least, in the fields – well my Dad put me into the pick-up and set me off driving down the road'. In relation to underage drinking 'thin' regulation is similarly apparent. This is explained by Kelly, a member of the Little Barning North Devon Young Farmers' Club focus group:

It's just generally the way you grow up. Like out here no-one's opposed to seeing a sixteen year old in a pub, in a country pub, on a week night, having the odd pint of beer or whatever, as long as they're sensible and the police don't really monitor it because its up to the landlord. In quiet villages you know everybody comes into your pub just about whereas it's more strict in towns with them enforcing everything.

Kelly's point is reiterated by the members of the Wexton Young Farmers' focus group in Northumberland:

Kath: I think we're more relaxed in the local pubs about serving people because we went out at quite a young age...there's our pub/

Celia: It doesn't shut until everyone goes home kind of thing.

Rob: But they know you're not going to do any harm, you're not doing any harm, you're just having a good laugh/

Celia: Yeah you're just having a good time/

Rob: Whereas people in town they get all worked up and start fighting.

Celia: I remember I walked out of there at eight o'clock in the morning and the local policeman was sitting outside!

[Laughter from the group]

Jeannie: That was after a special occasion. A private party.

Celia: And he was just like 'Morning, are you going home? Are you going that way?' And I went 'Yeah I'm going this way' and he went 'I'll go this way then' and I was like 'Thanks'. He went back later and had his breakfast at the pub with everyone else who was still there. He knew quite well that nothing was ever going to/

[The group breaks up into jokes about there being no police investigation]

This extract from the focus group conversation is significant because it offers an account of the ways in which everyday illegal practices – under-age drinking and the serving of alcohol outside licensing hours – are accommodated and it reveals the familiarity of the police officer with this participant – he knows where Celia lives for example – and he is part of the village – he joins the party for his breakfast. It is an example of the latitude of socio-legal governance in specific contexts. This latitude means that relatively minor illegal behaviours such as those described by the focus group can be incorporated and are normalised. This takes us back to the heterotopic argument concerning spaces of alternate ordering. These behaviours do not constitute transgressions that challenge their incorporation into everyday practices – for example Kelly, Celia and Rob all speak of highly constrained and regulated approaches to unregulated behaviour, of being sensible, of not doing any harm and only having a good time.

Another seeming paradox in the ways in which rural spaces can be interpreted was apparent in the third freedom discourse – that of the countryside being *over* regulated. As with the voices that valorised community and then spoke of the desire for the absence of people, the voices that claimed the rural as the site of freedom, as being valued as a space in which 'you can get away with loads' also claimed the rural as a site of intense socio-legal over-regulation.

Agricultural and land-use regulations, and the impact of these on rural practices, tended to be subject to expressions of animosity in both types of focus groups. Agriculture is a highly regulated industry, both at national government level but also European level, in terms of a complex system of grants and subsidies and requirements around livestock and land use. In this way there is a very direct relation between some people living in rural areas and high levels of bureaucratic legislation. In the UK this has seen an increase since the Foot and Mouth epidemic of 2002. The notion of thick bureaucratic regulation in rural areas is emphasised by extensive planning requirements concerning buildings and what can happen with land. Similarly as Foot and Mouth affected whole communities and the everyday movement of people and animals, it widened the regulatory experience of rural communities beyond those engaged in agriculture. What was common amongst participants was a perception of excessive rules and regulations or 'red tape'. This is explained by Great Easton WI focus group in North Devon, for example:

> Foot and Mouth has created tremendous change for those in the farming community. It's created all this horrendous paper work now and rules and regulations and Mrs Becket [Margaret Becket was Minister for Department of Farming, Environment and Rural Affairs at the time] and it's, it's made life much more difficult, particularly for those of us getting older in farming.

For many interviewees bureaucratic requirements were seen not only as an unjustified level of intervention, but as also eroding rural events and thereby rural freedoms and cultures. This can be heard in this conversation in this North Devon YFC group,

> Nathan: Every year we have a North Devon Field Day, and after Foot and Mouth we had to have licences for this, licences for that *instead of letting country people get on with themselves*.
>
> Sarah: I think it's had a lot less support as well because there's so much hassle organising it.
>
> Nathan: And if you do something wrong you end up in bloody court or something [...] you've got to be insured to do anything nowadays.
>
> Jacky: And I know as well that the Devon County Show where the whole county gets together, they've had problems with the animal restrictions for the stock judging haven't they?
>
> Nathan: That's what I mean. (Emphasis added)

It is the same sense of unfair, unknowledgable and external legislative demand which is present in the Green Leigh Northumberland YFC conversation,

> Richard: And we don't have a Leek Club anymore.
>
> Dan: Same with other agricultural shows though isn't it?
>
> Molly: There is no proper/
>
> Dan: No proper ones anymore.
>
> Sue: Is that because of Foot and Mouth?
>
> Jack: Yeah.
>
> Richard: And other things.
>
> Molly: There's so many regulations now.
>
> […]
>
> Annie: Since Foot and Mouth these people called English Nature sit in an office in London and my Dad always used quad bikes on the fell and they tell us we are not allowed to use them.
>
> Richard: There are so many restrictions on things.
>
> Annie: *They don't understand that you have to.*
>
> Molly: How are you going to get over/
>
> Annie: You can't walk around hundreds of miles.
>
> Richard: Well, it's just typical of people in towns making decisions.
>
> Someone: Exactly. *They're all out of touch with the countryside.*
>
> Richard: People in towns make decisions for us. (Emphasis added)

What clearly emerges from these conversations is a stress on locationality, the idea of a countryside culture and the desire (and ability) of rural communities to regulate themselves. Formal or juridical regulation is viewed here as excessive, external/outside, urban based, corrosive and nonsensical. Cohen found very similar sentiments as those being expressed in these focus group interviews in his study of the fishing blockade in Whalsay, in Shetland as Chapter 3 discussed. For example Cohen noted that there was 'the view that Shetland would fare quite satisfactorily if left to the Shetlanders: its problems result from the interference of outsiders. This self-confident insularity is a characteristic feature of the islanders' consciousness…Any breach of this insularity – say through the intervention of external authorities – is thus felt to be an impugnment of the integrity of local expertise and knowledge' (1982: 305).

It is with the return to the notion of self-regulating and bounded communities, captured by Ricky's argument for 'letting country people get on with it themselves' that it is possible to see the heterotopia of rurality i.e. a site of anti-orderly/freer spaces *and* a site of orderly/monitored spaces. Yet, there is a central compatibility to these two positions. Hetherington (1997) has stressed the need for the scrutiny of the *processes* of social ordering and in many ways while the processes of rural social order encountered in the research reveal their tensions and contradictions, their combined outcome is a self regulatory and, in this way, a *coherent* ordering of rural space. The desire for freedom; practising illicit behaviours; valuing the absence of social intervention and opposing (some) existing socio-legal intervention can all be accommodated in one narrative as long as they involve populations contained within the recognisable boundaries of community. This conditionality is about 'everybody knowing everybody and their business' *and* it is contingent upon ideas of who is considered to belong to particular spaces and who is not.

Conclusion

This chapter began with the claim that, despite a particular metanarrative, rural spaces do get invested with other, divergent, narratives. This can be seen as evidence of the 'never complete' or the 'unfinishedness' of the meaning of rurality. Remembering that this is a project which has focussed on processes of inclusion and those rural populations who appear to be able to make an unproblematic, dominant and familiar claim to rural belonging is a key element to this argument. While the existence of more than one rural story (sometimes told by the same voices) underlines the ambivalence of what the rural is, it is, at the same time, important to recognise that it was 'mainstream' and 'ordinary' rural voices that were articulating multiple and contradictory interpretations of rurality (see also Valentine, 1997). If there is dissent expressed by those who inhabit hegemonic rural identities this clearly unsettles any fixed or totalised definitions of what the rural is. The ambivalences that are exposed by this more broken narrative open up possibilities and create extra spaces for 'others' to be able to insert themselves and forge new rural narratives.

However, there is a need to be cautious about over-claiming the extent of such possibilities. Processes of social ordering in rural spaces can be analysed through the concepts of the panoptic and heterotopia. The panoptic captures the metanarrative of the thickly regulated rural. This is a space of community, order and the ever present regulatory gaze. Heterotopia speaks of simultaneously occurring other, or extra, rural spaces. These are thinly regulated spaces in which there is an absent or accommodating gaze. Clearly *some* of these contradictions were generationally shaped but more generally these contradictions also took place within and across generational and gender identities. While the concepts of the panoptic and of heterotopia illuminate the tensions between, and within, the divergent rural narratives, their shared focus on the production of order means that the incompatibilities are to a certain extent resolvable and certainly able to co-exist. We have seen the coherent management of contradiction throughout this chapter. For example it is evident in the ways in which participants thought of themselves as integral to their local communities but, at the same time, also desired isolation and not to see people; and in the ways in which young people could behave illegally – driving under age, driving over speed limits, drinking underage – but with some consent from the (local) adult world; or the ways in which participants valued order and the law, but resisted (what was perceived as) external authority and legal intervention. There is some resonance here with Valentine's study of parents' approaches to raising their children in the countryside where she found that 'the rural can be produced as simultaneously both safe and dangerous' (1997: 147). Valentine argues that this contradiction was managed by parents through an 'illusion of an "imagined community" in which they felt their children would always be safer than in urban environments' (ibid.: 146).

Again it is the ability of *community* to bind together multiple and contradictory strands that is striking (see Chapter 3). In mobilising community it is possible to see that the neighbourly, self-policing community exists for those who are included as members within its boundaries. The concept of the panoptic can be extended beyond the seeing or being seen dyad to include the *desire to be seen* and this desire for visibility itself becomes a form of community inclusion. What the focus group conversations show is the way in which the panoptic gaze is differently inflected and is able to distinguish between those familiars who are watched over and sometimes purposely *not* watched over and those 'unfamiliars' who are *always* watched out for. In this way familiarity and local neighbourly knowledges lend themselves to processes of self-regulation and self-policing. This process is able to incorporate the desires for freedom and unaccountability as well as illicit practices and, within the frames of the rural, the local, and above all, community, normalise all of these. In arguing that there is a particular logic evident in the processes of regulated and unregulated rural spaces it is possible to see a 'flattening out' of the rural as a heterotopic space. After all, it is within such flattened out, or strangely compatible tensions, that the regulated rural can assert its metanarrative status and undermine the unfinishedness of the countryside. However, that there are divergences as well as convergences in the ways in which rural spaces are interpreted and lived in is an argument I continue in the next chapter.

Chapter 7

Connecting Ruralities:
Alchemies of Ethnicity and Belonging

Introduction

The previous two chapters have been worrying about the ways in which community and countryside are *social* spaces. While the social continues to have a presence here what this chapter's worries centre around a return to those questions of ethnicity, identity and belonging raised earlier and more particularly to the relationship between these three categories and non-human things. In Chapter 3 I spent some time examining how ethnicity, Englishness and notions of home became bundled together in potent mixes of affirmation, loss and defensiveness. I want to continue in this chapter to think through ethnicity as, more than anything, an *alchemic* concept. I use the term 'alchemy' very deliberately. It is being used here to refer to the process of the mixing of different substances and also to flag the idea of transmutation and change. Following this my intentions in this chapter are twofold.

First, to continue to develop the suggestion that was begun in Chapter 2 – that formations of ethnicity draw on nature, on non-human things and, perhaps particularly draw on rural nature. As I argued earlier, despite the contested status of the category ethnicity, there tends to a shared consensus that it is the cultural and the social which provide the basis of ethnic identification and, unlike the category race, there has been a much more limited discussion as to the extent or ways in which ethnicity – and certainly majoritised ethnicities – mobilise and incorporate notions of the 'natural'. Of concern is to ask in what ways and through what hybrid markers the notions of ethnicity are given meaning in majoritised identity contexts and then to ask how stable and secure these markers are. In order to develop a response to these questions the application of actor-network theory (ANT) approaches – which stress the interdependence of the natural and the cultural – has been particularly useful. Using ANT as a way of understanding the project's data the chapter thinks through the ways in which the research participants invested the non-human, 'natural' world (hills, trees, plants, rivers, weather, seasons) with highly subjective national, local and intimate meanings each shaped by attachment and familiarity.

Second, the chapter examines how the process of imprinting ethnic meaning onto the non-human actors presents something of a paradox. In the first instance, as Chapter 3 argued, this process is problematic and conservative as it represents essentialist attempts to fix the boundaries of inclusion and recognition and in this way naturalise and nationalise ethnicity. However, the mobilisation of the non-human also creates openings and possibilities. The non-human may be re-read, it can be differently or diversely interpreted and it can offer routes through which new or reimagined ways of belonging can be formed. In many ways this paradox is a reflection of the task Stuart Hall urged at the beginning of the 1990s when he argued that,

> The real shift in the point of contestation is no longer only between antiracism and multiculturalism but inside the notion of ethnicity itself. What is involved is the splitting of the notion of ethnicity between, on the one hand the dominant notion which connects it to nation and race and on the other hand what I think is the beginning of a positive conception of the ethnicity of the margins, of the periphery. (1992: 78)

However, in Hall's conception of new ethnicities the predominant arenas of contestation and transformation were social and cultural whereas this chapter focuses on getting 'inside the notion of ethnicity' through the optics of the natural and the non-human – with all their social and cultural inflections.

The chapter begins with a brief review of the ways in which ethnicity and the commonly co-joined category race have both engaged and disengaged with notions of 'the natural'. While Chapter 3 discussed the idea of the primordial within ethnic formations this chapter looks at how social ideas of 'nature' get very specifically and instrumentally developed and used to explain and naturalise social divisions. It then considers the ways in which ANT offers insights into the ways in which these processes are constructed and mobilised. The chapter again draws on the project's data to investigate how the convergences between natural and social worlds appear in everyday discourses of ethnicity and ethnic meaning making and then moves to examine the possibilities of the natural and non-human to offer new and transformative routes of belonging, inclusion and attachment.

Ethnicity: The Social and the Natural?

As the language of 'race relations' falls, increasingly, into disuse – in the UK at least – and is replaced with the language of ethnicity this shift can be understood as a response to the problematic status of the concept of race and its categorisation of populations through phenotypical distinctions. This is reflected in Fenton's suggestion that 'the term "ethnic" has a much greater claim to analytical usefulness in sociology because it is not hampered by a history of connotations with discredited science and malevolent practice in the way the term race is' (1999: 4). While this argument seems to rather bypass the increasing number of ethnically related conflicts and political violence – perhaps most chillingly reflected in the term 'ethnic cleansing' – it is a persuasive suggestion. Although the terms race and ethnicity are often used interchangeably there is an implicit recognition that the term 'race' is one that refers to biology and physical appearances – particularly and persistently this has been skin colour but historically it has also included a range of other physical markers such as skull shape, hair type, and eye shape. In contrast ethnicity, reflecting its anthropological heritage, is understood as non-phenotypical and as a referent of the cultural – language, dress, religion, diet, custom and ritual. In their crudest reductive form then race and ethnicity can be read as drawing on 'the natural' and on the social respectively as their key sources. However, the ways in which the concept of race is framed within the idea of the natural is a process that is all social. The mobilisation of the natural in relation to race rather than ethnicity does not mean, as a number of commentators have noted, that the distinction between the two is discrete and bounded. Rather each constantly leaks into and is constitutive of the other. For example Hall (2000: 223) argues that,

> The biological referent is therefore never wholly absent from discourses of ethnicity, though it is more indirect. The more ethnicity matters the more its characteristics are represented as relatively fixed, inherent within a group, transmitted from generation to generation, not just by culture and education but by biological inheritance, stabilized above all by kinship and endogamous marriage rules that ensure that the ethnic group remains genetically and therefore culturally 'pure'.

From this Hall argues that there is a need to recognise the ways in which two converging 'logics or registers of racism' are produced and are simultaneously 'in play'. This echoes the arguments made in Chapter 3 about ethnic identification and the primordial. In other words, ethnicity, with its stress on culture, similarly presents a series of problematics not least the extent of the linkages between biologism of race and a cultural essentialisation of ethnicity – seen for example in ideas that culture is passed on and inherited; that ethnicity is fixed and that physical distinctions are folded into ascriptions of ethnic identities.

There is then every need to be wary of a preference for simply inserting ethnicity in place of race. Ethnicity complexly interacts with ideas of race but ethnicity offers a lens through which the social and emotional dimensions of culture and difference can be viewed and, in particular how these look to and incorporate the categories of the natural and rural nature. Chapter 3 began to set out why it is necessary to approach ethnicity as a process of identification and ascription which looks socially to the natural world. And while the role of the natural and biology has been problematised and extensively critiqued in relation to race (see Miles, 1989; Anthias and Yuval-Davis, 1992; Malik, 1996; St. Louis, 2002 for example) the notion of the natural in relation to ethnicity, has with few exceptions (see Billig,

1995; Hall, 2002; Balibar, 1991 for example), not been extensively addressed and the role of rural nature even less so. For example Fenton has emphasised the importance of setting ethnicity in political and economic contexts in order to understand that 'ethnicity is manifested as a dimension of cultural meanings and as a dimension of social structure: ethnic formations are material, symbolic and social facts' (1999: xi). However this falls someway short of recognition of the processes of the naturalisation of ethnic formation. Closer to my own intentions is Balibar's (1991) argument for the term 'fictive ethnicity' by which he means the ways in populations are categorised and/or described 'as if they form a natural community possessing of itself an identity of origins, culture and interests which transcends individuals and social conditions' (cited in Hutchinson and Smith, 1996: 164). It is from this that Balibar (ibid.) raises the pertinent questions as to: 'how can ethnicity be produced? And how can it be produced in such a way that it does not appear as fiction, but as the most natural of origins?' Balibar argues that this naturalisation takes place through language and through notions of race but it extends to and incorporates particular spaces and landscapes through which to purchase ethnic (and national) identity. I, along with other commentators, have argued that rural spaces have been particularly selected in narratives of English nationhood as a potent site in which ethnic meaning and its 'naturalisation' can be assembled (Wright, 1984; Agyeman and Spooner, 1997; Matless, 1998; Neal, 2002; Neal and Agyeman, 2006).

However, this work on the spatial securing of Englishness has tended to be concerned with the exclusionary dynamics of the securing process and analysed in relation to be what Fenton would call macro, ethnic national identity. Quite rightly rural studies and ethnicity commentators have emphasised the effective folding of nation into rural and the ways in which particular populations and figures then become silenced, effaced, and/or problematised within that process (ibid.; Cloke and Little, 1997). But what has been less discussed are the ways in which small scale, intimate, locally embedded discourses and practices of identity formation and ethnic sense making look to – or depend on – an interaction with non-human factors and 'natural' environments. Chapter 3 began to think this through and set out the ways in which Englishness draws consistently on rural nature in an attempt to find both a core image and a mirror of what it is. But as with all mirrors the reflections were fleeting and unstable and liable to other revelations.

The relationality between the social and the natural – and in particular the ethnic and emotional meanings that the non-human entities can become invested with – has led me to ANT. The paucity in the analysis of ethnicity formations through the lens of ANT is surprising as, as both Hall and Balibar have noted, ethnicity operates through a social–natural hybrid. Recent calls in sociological debates have been keen to stress the need for the discipline itself to re-engage with the natural and more specifically with the natural sciences (see also Fuller, 2006 and Rose, 2007). Skinner (2007: 940) has, for example, argued that late 20th-century sociology, in its efforts to distance itself from any early biological and evolutionary legacies has, as a consequence, 'lost an interest in the relationship between nature and culture and an appreciation that social life is neither independent of biology nor can it be reduced to biology'. While it is not the intention here to look to the biological *per se* it is the call to go *beyond* the social when examining the social that is pertinent here and what is empirically attempted in the chapter's consideration of what social–nature relations 'look like' as they manifest themselves and are articulated in everyday discourses and meaning-making around place and ethnic identification.

It is not my intention to rehearse the extensive body of work that is associated with ANT (Latour, 1993; Callon, 1998; Law, 1994; Whatmore, 2002). Rather my intention here is to borrow some key elements from ANT and transfer them, via the consideration of empirical data, to the argument that processes of ethnic sense making rely on the mobilisation of notions of nature and the natural. In this way I can ask first, how rural nature gets practiced in formations of ethnicity and explanations of local belonging and second I can ask how rural nature itself shapes those practices and feelings about places and attachment. Developed out of the theorisation of the relation between the social and technology perhaps the most relevant and pertinent contributions that ANT offers is the central emphasis it places on the interdependency and interactions of the human and the non-human and the challenges, if not the impossibilities, of modernism's attempts to 'purify' the distinction between or maintain the separateness of nature/non-humans and culture/ humans. If a proximate, inter-relationship rather than a discrete, distance between the human and the non-human is accepted then the concept of networks or constant combinations of humans and things offers different ways into understanding the social and the cultural – as nature–cultures (Hinchliffe, 2007). As Latour explains, the idea of a network is appealing because 'it is more supple than the notion of a system, more historical than the notion of structure, more empirical than the notion of complexity, the idea of the network is Ariadne's thread of these interwoven stories' (1989: 3). At its heart ANT argues that nothing can act in an isolated vacuum – all heterogenous social, natural, technological entities must bump into each other in some form to produce an action, practice, effect and so forth in an ever unstable and ever proximate and intersecting relation between an actor and the network. ANT has been valuable in that it provides an approach which does not view the natural and the social as distinct or pure binary categories but as a co-constituted, translating hybrids or crossings (Hinchliffe, 2007) which 'are mobilized and assembled into associative networks in which the collective capacity for human/non-human action is expressed [... and] all manner of things constantly combine and recombine in the formation of the functioning world' (Cloke, 2003: 5).

The second key aspect of ANT which is closely related to the above and which is useful to the suggestion of an alchemic process within formations of ethnicity is ANT's emphasis on the agency not only of humans but crucially of the non-human, of things. The idea of the agency of things has to be placed in the context of ever connected, combining networks of the human practices, knowledges and emotions that take place and emerge through encounters and relations with the non-human. In this way animals, plants, trees, buildings, hills, rivers, the weather and so on can each and all become aligned and entangled with – and, importantly, influence – what humans do and feel and experience (see Cloke and Jones, 2003).

A quick example from a memory. It is a hot day in the park in the summer. My baby, newly born, is fractious and crying in his pushchair. Flustered – is he hungry? Is he too hot? Is he ill? – I see a sycamore tree whose big branches and leaves offer protection from the sun. In this way the tree invites me to go a sit for a while within/under its coolness – which I do and I can feed my baby and then the two of us both feel calmer from our resting under the tree. And I remember that day, that is now years ago. The tree and how it gave hospitality and shady comfort stays with me – I feel affection for it when I pass it now. Or another example. I am with my lover on campus and we want to kiss and hold each other but the open publicness of where we are inhibits us. We going are going to drive to have lunch and so we walk to his car. There is a beech hedge that surrounds the car park and we sit in the car which is parked next to the hedge. These two things offer us a sense of privacy and we are able to kiss each other! These may seem like simplifying vignettes but they do capture the ways in which the human and the non-human combine and how human behaviour gets shaped and affected by this *inter-relational* agency. The tree and the shade that the tree made produced an action, a response from me and an engagement with me. The combination of the car and the hedge offered protection from being viewed, influenced human practices and allowed me to be kissed. I am now connected to the hedge. I smile to myself when I walk past it. The hedge is part of my story. In this way my behaviour and experiences and the non-human things in my surrounds combine and are creatively co-constituted. These are also intimate vignettes. This is deliberate because my intention is to keep the emotional in focus as it reminds us that how we 'are' in spaces and places involves the human and the non-human being continually enrolled and assembled in richly personal and individual as well as public and collective ways. I return to this in the discussions below (see also Chapter 3).

ANT approaches have been particularly taken up by rural studies scholars (see Cloke and Jones, 2001; Cloke 2003 for example) as rural spaces most readily offer an interactive arena in which nature–social relationship is most explicitly visible i.e. a space in which the natural and the social are so intimate and proximate that it does not make analytical sense to see them as separate (MacNaughten and Urry, 2001; Murdoch, 2003: 264–5). The receptiveness of rural studies to ANT thinking can also be understood within the context of rurality's pre-modern associations which has threaded through the previous chapters. If modernism attempted to purify and create distinct bounded categories of nature, social, science, politics then rural environments and cultures present some of the most obvious challenges to this. This is not to say that processes of purification have not been applied to rural spaces of course. Some of the most dramatic and frightening examples of the 'dangers' of the purification attempts and the modernist denial of the relationality of nature–culture–science have been rurally related – Avian Flu, Foot and Mouth disease, BSE and so forth. Such events and threats can be understood as emerging as disruptive 'quasi objects' out of separatist approaches to the human and non-human (Hinchliffe, 2007: 97). While ANT may have been embraced by rural scholars in order to explain rural social relations and while it may have been ignored by ethnicity studies there has been a concern for the latter, as my previous work on the rural spaces of England has shown, with the enrolment and mobilisation of these particular 'nature–culture' spaces in the representational securing of a majoritised English cultural identity (Neal, 2002; Neal and Agyeman, 2006; Chapter 3).

However, there has been a stress in this work on the ways in which the countryside is assembled so as to work as a key social referent for ethnic identity formation and national belonging. This work has tended to argue that certain landscapes are very deliberately and consciously deployed to influence politicised social processes such as inclusion and exclusion. But, as Murdoch (2003), citing Whatmore has argued, the countryside is 'more than human' and so it is not possible to straightforwardly suggest that primacy can be given to the social project of instrumentally 'using' nature to secure political processes. Rather the emphasis can be more usefully placed on the hybridity and the crossings, of the social and the natural within efforts to secure and stabilise narratives of nation and belonging as this 'has the potential to capture socio-natural complexity of the countryside more easily than traditional modes of representation' (ibid.: 264). In this way it is important to note that the relation between ethnic identity formation and the countryside is not straightforwardly the social + the rural nor is it simply that the social is reflected in the rural but rather that social identities (and ethnic formations) take place '*through* and *within* rural nature' (ibid.: 278. Original emphasis). It is to this that the chapter now turns.

Nature–Culture Hybridity: Place Attachments and Ethnicity

Cloke and Jones (2001: 650) use the notion of dwelling in order to extend and develop the ANT-influenced explanations of how human and non-human natural entities combine and are active in the constructions and formations of places. They suggest that 'dwelling is about the rich intimate ongoing togetherness of beings and things which make up landscapes and places and which bind together nature and culture over time' (ibid.: 651). It was with this idea of dwelling in mind – and in particular the emotional intimacy of human ties to non-human entities and elements of places – which the three extracts from different focus group interview conversations that are cited below seem to directly speak.

Lizzie: When I open my curtains I keep seeing all the fields and great big trees and I like that. I would prefer to open my window to that rather than buildings.

Researcher: Can you say anything about why you like that view – why is because its not buildings?

Lizzie: It just looks natural and it is part of the place where you live.

Researcher: That's important for you?

Lizzie: Yes.

Phoebe: It's a bit like Lizzie cos outside my window there's just like millions of fields and when it's snowy it's really nice and white and its just where the sun is so you can see the sun rise in the morning. (Whitely Chapel YFC)

Researcher: [To Lorraine who has moved to the village from London] Where did you get the feeling you wanted to live in the countryside?

Lorraine: I don't know – I wanted a bigger garden, I wanted fields – it was just something, perhaps it was in my genes.

Linda: I think you feel freer somehow don't you?

Beatrice: Yes and the quiet, peace and quiet, to see the stars, the weather/

Linda: The stars that you can see and the fields, yeah.

Researcher: Tell me more about why that appeals to you, what's special about it?

Sheila: I don't know – just because you can see a long way. You can see the country, the fields growing/

Linda: /you get to see the weather coming in don't you? (Peter's Green WI)

Geraldine: There are a lot of small valleys in Northumberland that themselves are absolutely precious. You know just as you go round a corner you come into a another valley and it's just so gorgeous/

Bessie: At one part of the road when you're going up to Allandale the whole area just opens up and its marvelous, the views/

Doreen: /and the cotton grass growing.

Bessie: Yes, Yes.

Doreen: Well you see you get hooked on the flora, that's the trouble. Well it has me anyway, I mean I go and look to make sure the plants are still there where I'd seen them years ago. (Dilston WI)

Each of these conversations shows how participants' affinities to their localities were defined and valued through a discourse of rural nature. It is the non-human entities – stars, sun, weather, trees, fields, plants – that are all work as emotional symbols of attachment and affection. Consider for example Geraldine's description of the valleys as 'absolutely precious' and the rest of the group's agreement with her. Doreen talks of being 'hooked' on the plants and in a similarly intimate way Lizzie talks of her pleasure at what she sees from her bedroom window and the view being 'part of the place' where she lives. In these accounts it is natural 'organic' entities that are directly selected and drawn on to describe how participants related to their surrounds. And these entities are favourably compared to what are seen here as the limits of what social worlds can offer. In other words, for these participants it is the absence of buildings, people, noise and such that is appreciated and sought. This articulation of a valuing of a proximity to rural nature and being in the natural world was expressed across both age and gender lines. There is a remarkable symmetry between the descriptions of attachment in the Young Farmers Club interview and those of the two Women's Institutes interviews. While the above extracts all cite female participants the expression and explanation of participants' attachments to locality by drawing on nature was not gendered. It was also regularly expressed by the male participants in the Young Farmers Clubs. It is clearly present for example in Stuart's detailed description of where he enjoys being,

> There's a place up on top of the fells, there's a big long crag and you can stand on top of the crag and its thirty feet to the bottom and you just look up fell and it changes and you've got trees at the top and you've got one kind of grass to the left and to the right…its always changing, you can see it in the snow, you can see it in summer, its just quiet and its about two miles from any building.

There is a sense of time coming through in these accounts. This is mainly measured by the seasons and how these make the landscapes alter but is also there in the references to plants and the return of plants and their growing again as Doreen's comment about needing to go and make sure that the plants have come back and 'are still there' where she'd seen them years ago. As Richard Mabey argues in *Nature Cure* 'plants are part of what makes a locality, differentiates it, makes an amorphous site into a place, a territory, an address' (2006: 152). Time is important to the notion of dwelling – Cloke and Jones speak of dwelling being 'the recognition of time-deepened experience…the richness of things over time' (2001: 654) for example. However – and crucially, the identification of rural nature as the means through which place affection and attachment are developed and sustained is not contingent on the longevity of, or a 'born and bred', place relation. For example, while Doreen's return over years to look at and check on the plants does emphasise the longevity of her presence in the locality Lorraine's comments illustrate a very similarly expressed affinity and yet Lorraine had only recently moved into the village. It is interesting that Lorraine explains her rationale for her move from the city to the country and through a naturalistic reference – the need to be in a rural space was 'in her genes'.

This affirmation of strong attachment to place *without* a longevity of presence brings us back to the findings of Savage et al. (2005) in terms of the importance of the local for their key concept of 'elective belonging' which was first discussed in Chapter 3. Elective belonging is used by Savage et al. as a conceptual descriptor of the process by which in-migrants, non-resident or mobile populations can 'articulate senses of spatial attachment […] and forms of connectivity' (2005: 29) to a particular locality. In their study Savage et al. focus on their participants' biographies and they ways in which they 'account to themselves how they come to live where they do'. Savage et al. examine the social and cultural practices and values of their participants and show how these are inflected and reflective of their local attachments. With their research set in the Northwest England – four locations in and around Manchester – their study focuses predominantly on social and cultural networks – work, friends, schools, leisure, neighbourhoods – and does not address the non-human elements of place belonging – although some participants in a semi rural location did describe their attachment in terms of their access to the surrounding rural landscapes. Savage et al. argue that 'one's residence is a crucial, possibly the crucial identifier of who you are. The sorting processes by which people chose to live in certain places and others leave is at the heart of contemporary battles over social distinction' (2005: 207). It is exactly the work that non-human entities do in these 'sorting processes' and the ways in which they relate to rural identity and rural place affinity that the data discussed here illuminates.

The notion of elective belonging, presenting as it does a direct conceptual and empirical challenge to notions of primordial 'born and bred' and 'indigenous' belonging coupled with ANT's simultaneous emphasis on natural and the social crossings – offer something that is useful to ethnicity studies and is a response to Hall's urgings to prise open ethnicity. And there are possibilities for opening up ethnicity – people may elect the ways in which to make sense of their relation to/ affection for particular locations and we have already seen how nature is centrally integrated into this sorting process. It is the intensely *social* basis of this that underlines the instability of such processes and highlights the possibilities of other claims to be purchased. The social–natural crossings are unpredictable and have the potential to be turbulently constituted as the politics of rurality discussed in Chapters 1 and 2 evidence.

Any focus on the ways in which nature and society are able to reinforce each other in relation to the formations of ethnic identity has to take into account the 'fixing work' that the natural and the social hybrid can do in processes of securing ethnic identity and notions of nation. For example, a central pattern in the data from the project was the way in which participants used nature and the natural environment not only to situate their locationality and place attachment but also, and at times simultaneously, make connective threads to national identity. I introduced some of this in Chapter 3 and the following extracts all draw on similar but distinct aspects of non-human nature to illustrate this connectivity:

Pam: We think of the English countryside as very green and it used to have a lot of trees [...] when you go towards the hall there's the most beautiful field with lovely mature trees scattered throughout the field and to me that's just an English scene. I think there is something about English – I mean Northern Europe I suppose – you get trees as well there don't you? But there's not the lushness I think that you get here is there?

Nancy: We had some friends staying with us a good few years ago from Australia. It was the first time she had been over here and the thing that she and Mark kept saying is 'look at the fields they're so small, they're just like patchwork'. And that's the thing I like about our countryside. I always think how nice it is. It's typically English, the little fields. (Ugham WI)

This conversation deploys three now familiar relational markers of Englishness – greenery, trees and fields. While the citing of trees in this way is not surprising – there is of course a long history of trees signifying national spaces and stories and the complex emotional relationship between people and trees has been examined by Cloke and Jones (2003) – what is important is the *extent* of the work that trees and fields have to do in terms of offering a shorthand for both personal attachment to place and in being enrolled into standing in for collective ethnic identity. However, it is important to note Pam's uncertainty as she moves from claiming the description she gives the group as an 'English scene' to broadening it out to Northern Europe and then moves back to suggesting that it could be the very green exuberance of the trees that identifies them as unquestionably English. Nancy's response is both an affirmation of her agreement with Pam and a development of her strategy of defining Englishness through nature and against other national spaces. This comparative thinking resonates with the suggestion made by Savage et al. that, 'elective belonging is critically dependent on people's relational sense of place, their ability to relate their area of residence against other possible areas' (2005: 29). It is interesting however, that while Savage et al. found 'identities are developed through networked geography of places articulated together' (ibid.: 208) and that this network was multi-scale – it was local, regional and global but 'one of the striking and largely unexpected findings from our research was the *limited significance* of the national frame of reference in people's cultural imaginations'(ibid. Emphasis added). There is a difference with my project of course – the participants were being directly asked about Englishness and they did make a series of connections between the rural nature–culture and national identity. We have seen this in the data discussed above and in Chapter 3 and it emerges, for example in the following interview conversation:

Annette: That's country life though because you've got your seasons and on a farm you've got your stock and lambs being born/

Iris: Spring every year/

Susan: That's particularly English what you talked about/

Annette: The outdoor life?

Susan: The outdoor life but the changing seasons.

Iris: All these things to look forward to whereas if you live abroad in Spain or Cyprus every season is the same, it's just all the same.

Mary: My sister used to say when she lived in Australia, its always wearing the same clothes, whereas in England we have our spring clothes, our summer clothes, our autumn clothes and our winter thick woollies.

Susan: That's right.

Mary: She said 'I'm so sick of seeing men in shorts all the year round. Never a decent pair of trousers on'.

Iris: The seasons/

Susan: /Yes, the seasons.

The various strands of dialogue here are all effectively pulled together by the end of the conversation to define Englishness. The equation of 'country' or 'outdoor life' into Englishness and the comparative frame echoes – even down to the use of Australia – the defining criteria of Englishness used in the earlier interview extract. But it is the group's agreement on seasons as representing and being Englishness that is notable. This is not because this conversation ignores that other places/national spaces have seasons but because seasons offers so *slight* an 'architecture' around which to build ethnic identity. The slightness of not only seasons and weather but *all* of these markers – trees, field patterns, greenery – is important because, more than anything, it exposes the emotional but more the *ephemeral* heart of ethnicity. This is to return to the arguments of Chapter 3 and Patrick Wright's emphasis on the need to recognise the 'vagueness of deep England'. In some ways then the absence of the national frame for the participants in Savage et al.'s study did mirror the challenges participants encountered in mine. Yes, participants spoke of Englishness and made efforts to connect it to and define it through rural nature but their success in doing this was not clear. The richer and emotional expressions of connection tended to be to locale and to their everyday environments. This is in no way to suggest that the elusive or vague 'things' that are selected to constitute Englishness make the ethnic sense making any less durable or effective. Clearly they do not. What is illuminated is the way in which processes of identification enroll non-human entities that are unpredictable and not straightforwardly compliant with social and political projects. This may, if not equally but nevertheless possibly, create transformative opportunities and openings and it is these that I now want to consider.

Nature–Culture Hybridity: A Way of Opening up Ethnicity?

There is a strange duality, or sleight of hand, since the assembling of non-human things to create, mark, make sense of and secure place and ethnic attachment can also emphasise the instability and insecurity of those very same efforts. This brings me back to the proposition that ANT is a helpful tool for analysing ethnic formations although this is not a carte blanch embrace. As Cloke (2003: 6–7) worries, what does ANT offer politically – 'for example how does a recognition of hybridity and embodied practice help address issues of social exclusion and spatial purification? How do these different ways of knowing rurality suggest answers to issues of political and ethnical priority? How do they equip us to do anything about anything?' Similarly Cloke and Jones (2001) argue that the idea of dwelling needs some care so as to avoid its associations with a romanticised, bounded fixidity and the evocation of primordialism which Chapter 3 examined. In this final part of the chapter what I want to do is to try and think through the ANT cautions that Cloke and Jones raise via an idea that nature–culture–social crossings are able to present opportunities for recasting ways of belonging (see also Murdoch, 2003). These opportunities may be unpredictable and uncertain but what the basic tenets of ANT allow or create space for is a focus on how identity formation processes which draw on non-human entities may be re-read by others and then used not only as boundary markers to exclude and deny others but as sites for inclusive and/or transformative attachments and affinities.

To think through this idea I am going to return to the work of Michael Bell which I discussed in Chapter 2. Bell noted that Childerley, the village he studied, was strongly marked by class divisions and social and economic status. While this was openly acknowledged by residents to Bell, they were morally troubled by it: 'the contradiction that Childerleyans have most spoken about in this book is their ambiguous feelings about class and material motivations' (1994: 230). Bell argues that this unease about social divisions in the village was contained – to some extent – by a discourse of community (see Chapter 3) but, more interestingly (in terms of this chapter) and more affectively, these divisions were both undermined and transcended by a common claiming and shared affinity to having, more than anything else, a rural identity. This identity was rooted in Bell's participants' attachment to and love of the countryside and their development of a 'natural conscience'. The idea of a natural conscience meant that the residents of the village could move beyond social interests and the moral and political tensions and uncomfortableness that those created and instead 'construct a sense of a *natural me* […] the *me* of being a country person' (ibid.: 239. Original emphasis). As Jonathan Murdoch neatly summarises,

> Bell believes the security of the country identity derives from proximity to nature. Through this proximity the villagers manage to connect themselves to the natural environment…Thus an affiliation with the countryside [all] villagers

can achieve a secure moral foundation for their lives: affluent and poor 'gain a secure place in the "natural order" of the countryside'. (2003: 277)

Bell's arguments as to how identities can, through the entangled strands of the social and natural, become transformed bears much relevance to my arguments. If there is some, albeit, limited evidence of nature unsettling and transforming class based social identities and divisions when it is part of a network process then how might this work specifically in terms of ethnicity? Bell himself notes how 'in this [his] book I have emphasised the undermining of class, but the same could probably be said of religion, gender and race, at least in some places' (1994: 240).

Clearly I have been arguing here, and across the previous chapters, that rural nature is sometimes emotionally and sometimes instrumentally drawn on in various social, cultural and everyday ways to define and secure Englishness and belonging. In many ways I am following Hetherington's work here. In his research with New Age Travellers Hetherington discusses the ways in which they reinterpret rural Britain in order to shed their suburban backgrounds and make new identities,

> The Celtic fringe, pagan sites and the unspoilt English countryside are the antithesis of the idea of suburbia. They are, in particular, the spaces of an earlier, largely forgotten British ethnicity waiting to be reclaimed. The ideas of identity and a constructed ethnicity are mapped out in a distinct way of seeing the landscape. The spaces that Travellers occupy are spaces of identity [...] not only are identities created through the practices of festivals and travel in the countryside, but the imaginary geography of the rural is also a source in the making of this identity. It is the margins, the mysterious and forgotten parts of the British Isles, with which the Travellers identify. (2006: 181–2)

Hetherington's work shows that rural nature can be invested with and used to purchase different or transformative ethnic meaning. However, New Age Travellers represent explicitly counter cultural figures and their presence and attempts to reclaim and write new ethnic formations into English rural landscapes have been bitterly contested (see Chapter 2). But there are other, although still only limited evidential sources, from which to empirically argue that the undermining or re-reading and opening up of Englishness through rural nature is possible and occurs on a 'quieter' scale than the New Age Traveller controversies. However, that which is available supports the notion of the re-reading of rural spaces. The largely small scale qualitative access focused research regularly records research participants explaining their pleasure of being in the English countryside as being partially constructed through reflective memory – in which these rural spaces can be read as other rural spaces and national places. For example, in her research on visible communities relationship to the countryside, and to English National Parks in particular, Kye Askins found that a number of her participants were sympathetic to the relationship between Englishness and rurality and saw mirrors of this in the place of the countryside in other narratives of nation such as India, the Caribbean, Pakistan and Ghana. Askins explains that,

> This allowed individuals to develop attachment to the English countryside via connections between one rural landscape and another, and participants discussed visiting places that reminded them of countries of (parental) origin. The Lake District and Peak District in particular were often linked to both the Himalayan foothills and the Blue Mountains in Jamaica. Such links went beyond the visual sense too, with people describing sounds and smells as indicative of other places. (2006: 165)

There is a *transnational* dimension to rural spaces being alluded to in Askins' findings. This can also be seen in the observation made by the journalist Graham Coster when he observed how, 'A day's pony trekking for migrant Muslim girls in the Brecon Beacons reminded everyone of Kashmir and Mirpur where they used to live. The small villages, the streams, the green fields…you feel just like you're at home'" (cited in Darby, 2000: 246). Similarly Claire Rishbeth's account of the recent migrant perceptions of, and reflections on, nature, green and open spaces in Sheffield and in the countryside around the city also reveal processes of re-reading. Rishbeth in particular details the ways in which the plants in Sheffield's Botanical Gardens, many of which being globally sourced, were familiar to the participants and made immediate connections with home and were responded to with 'a complex mix of pleasure, sadness and pride' (2006). The project visited two rural spaces outside Sheffield – a woodland and a heathland. Both of these spaces had affinities for the participants. Rishbeth discusses how the heathland in particular with its rocky outcrops and silver birch trees reminded participants from African countries of those countries. Rishbeth quotes from Farmina, one of the participants in her project, who finds an instant familiarity in the features of this Yorkshire landscape and her country of departure describing the heathland as being 'just like Rwanda….I never thought I could find a place like this in this country'. What is especially relevant from the Rishbeth study in terms of my arguments is the global re-reading of landscape and of familiarity and similarity which this re-reading is contingent upon. As Rishbeth puts it, 'through our personal world-views not only can Pembrokeshire be like Cornwall but also Chile like Norway and even Rwanda like Yorkshire.'

Global and transnational re-readings and claimings of landscapes and nature and so emotionally investing in them is not a recent phenomenon. Nor, as the New Age Traveller phenomenon shows, is it confined to migrants and minority populations within receiving countries For example Wendy Darby details a number of colonial accounts that reveal how landscapes in India, Sri Lanka, Tasmania, New Zealand were seen as the English Lake District: 'the scenery around Newtown [Tasmania] is the most beautiful I have seen this side of the world – very much resembling that of the Cumberland Lakes: the broad and winding Derwent flows between lofty and picturesque hills and mountains…It seemed like being on the right side of the world again' (Meredith, 1852 cited in Darby, 2000: 90). Re-reading England onto this colonised landscape went further than simply experiencing this association, writing about and painting them. In a reflection of the colonial process itself Darby discusses how Kandy, a valley city in the centre of mountainous Sri Lanka which also lent itself to association with the Lake District was then physically modeled on a Lake District panorama with promenades, carriage drives and riding paths constructed and vegetation cleared so as to establish Lake District styled viewing points (ibid.). The colonial (often literal) 'superimposing' of a 'home' landscape on colonised 'other' landscapes works as another reminder that nature is never just nature and returns us to ANT and its emphasis on the hybrid mix of the social and the natural.

In my research project, despite the selection of nature as the key referent for explaining their own affinity to their rural locality and as a key referent for defining those spaces as English and Englishness, there *was* a widespread recognition that nature was constantly combined with social processes as these extracts show:

> Faye: Things don't just stay green. You drive around and see farmers who've taken set aside [EU initiative whereby farmers are paid a grant to completely leave the land unfarmed] and their land is a mess. You've only got to go to Chumleigh [the next village] and it's just one mess.
>
> Researcher: What makes it a mess?
>
> Clifford: Because it's just allowed to grow and nothing is done to it…you wouldn't be able to take picture post cards – it's just converting back to scrubland, wilderness. (Alverdiscott YFC)

> Rachel: Well I think people [non-farming people] think it's [countryside] going to be a perfect little place where they've got all the green grass and cows out in the field/
>
> Richard: /they just picture it like it is in the spring and summer.
>
> Rachel: /and they don't actually realize the hard work that goes into it. They don't realize you have to plough a field to get it back into being grass again or they don't realize that you have to spread muck onto the field or put fertilizer on it or anything like that and they don't know that you have to get up at half past five and milk cows or do the sheep or whatever. (Whitely Chapel YFC)

While there is a critical tone to these conversations as the participants' comment on the lack of rural knowledge and/or appreciation of the human labour that goes into 'making' countryside what is more significant is the way in which these conversations acknowledge the social and natural inter-relationship. In short the criticism can be read as more than the failure of some people to realise the amount of human effort that produces many of the emotionally pleasing and socially meaningful aspects of rural nature. Some of this effort is predominantly economically driven as in the Northumberland and Devon YFCs interviews and it is at times aesthetically driven as in 19th-century Sri Lanka. It is then possible to read the criticism in the extracts as recognition of the hybrid, co-constituting relationality of the social and the natural. As Murdoch (2003: 279 original emphasis) notes 'the countryside continues to be shaped by social processes, it is just that these processes are *more than* social (just as the countryside continues to be shaped by natural processes that are *less than* natural)'.

Conclusion

This chapter has been concerned to show that the analysis of ethnicity – a category which tends to be overwhelmingly conceptualised as social – needs to begin attend to the ways in which it incorporates and inter-relates with the natural world. This is not to deny the work and discussions that have taken place regarding the ways that ethnicity is inflected with biologist discourses which essentialise and fix cultural and social practices, use and rely on physical markers to identify and ascribe populations to ethnic groups and the stress an intergenerational and inherited notion of ethnicity. Indeed at the beginning of the chapter I argued that the category of race in particular, but also ethnicity, illustrate *par excellence* modernist attempts to separate and purify science and politics, nature and culture and the malevolent and instrumental intentions and outcomes of this process. As John Solomos (1996) reminds us the concept of race comes from racism rather than processes of racism being a product of the existence of 'race'.

It is because of the ways in which ethnicity works simultaneously through a nature–culture relation that ANT offers potentially helpful perspectives through which to extend ethnicity studies. And while ANT has been drawn on somewhat selectively here it has been its focus on non-purified nature–culture crossings that has been especially emphasised. What has been suggested here is that by thinking of ethnicity as an *alchemic* assemblage of identity it emphases the ways in which all manner of human and non-human things get mobilised and enrolled to secure those formations. The range of empirical data used in this chapter illuminate the ways in which it was the non-human which was richly and intimately used by participants as ways of defining and explaining their attachment to the places in which they lived. Seasons, weather, hills, trees, fields, plants, views were read as emotionally and spatially meaningful and provided an everyday, (sometimes) time-deepened, means through which ontological security could be purchased and reaffirmed. Bringing together ANT and ethnicity studies also provides some room to think through the emotional and intimate aspects of ethnic formations. As Chapter 3 discussed processes of ethnic identification are both individual and collective. As this chapter has argued ANT, and ANT extended concepts such as dwelling, provide optics for analysing the intimate combinations and engagements between human and non-human things that ethnic formations alchemically bundle together.

This alchemic bundling provides ways in which to affirm locationality and it is also used to define and secure national ethnic identity and Englishness. Again ANT offers a relevant and valuable emphasis on the multidimensionality of nature. Nature animates and is animated in unpredictable and insecure ways. For example, people are able to rapidly construct bonds with places without any longevity of presence and the ability to do this can often be explained through the work of non-human things on human senses. Placing such non-human entities such as seasons, weather, greenery, fields, views at the heart of ethnicity claiming reveals the emphemerality of ethnicity and presents opportunities through which ethnicity can be unsettled. In other words what could be claimed as archetypically English can be constantly re-read and reinterpreted as a referent for another place and national space and it allows and engenders attachment and affection. Thinking of ethnicity as nature–culture crossings means considering how nature shapes *and* can *unshape* ethnic identities. The alchemic process in which the human and the non-human are combined to produce narratives or fictions of ethnicity can, and do, act as potent exclusionary markers. However, it is this hybridity or alchemy that lends the process a particular instability and provides the continual possibility of reinterpretation and more diverse claimings. As this chapter has shown, nature–culture intersections thread through discourses of attachment. These operate as a sites and arenas for securing ethnic formation but, at the same time, it has been shown that the multidimensionality of ANT means that it may be possible to see that processes of ethnic formation are curiously – and hopefully – wide open.

Chapter 8
Conclusion

Introduction

I began this book with Esra's story about not being able to answer the nature quiz questions in her new school about the names of the trees and plants in the new country to which her family had migrated. And I notice as I write this the popular rural lifestyle magazine *Country Living* is running a 'Bring Back the Nature Table' campaign. The campaign states that 'we want to see a nature table in every primary school, and urge parents, grandparents and guardians to take children regularly to explore local parks, woodlands and fields' (2008: 58). Susy Smith, *Country Living*'s editor explains that 'displaying a collection of natural finds in the classroom elevates them to *something special* – an art form – and allows children to contribute by bringing in things they may have found with their parents. And as the items are labelled even the youngest children start to learn the words for them and accept them as *something of importance*. I suspect the nature table has just fallen out of fashion and I believe it is time we made it cool again, especially in *urban schools* where they don't have the luxury of a lot of green space around them' (2008: 9. Emphasis added). While national identity is not mentioned at all in the campaign it is hard not to see it haunting around the peripheries of the unexplained argument that being able to recognise nature is 'special' and 'important' and especially so for urban children. Esra's experience of not being able to do this reinforced her sense of outsiderness, of not belonging to the nation. This book has in many ways been an exploration of Esra's story. It is a story that examines the work that rural nature does in social relations and to processes of inclusion and exclusion within ethnic and national formations and identifications.

The book also began with Conor and Louise Taaffes' intensely moving account of how they had responded to being witnesses to the murder of Stephen Lawrence. Esra's fragment of a childhood memory and the Taaffe's pouring of the water with Stephen's blood in it onto their rose bush both show that the nature–social relation is an emotional, intimate and personal one as well as a political and collective one. I have tried to keep the notion of intimacy as a thread running through all of the chapters here because, as Liz Bondi reminds us, 'telling our stories – narrating events of our lives – is an ordinary and necessary practice in many cultures. Many of us feel the need to do this in relation to many different events, especially ones in which we are emotionally invested whether as a result of trauma or for more ordinary processes of confirming, sustaining and creating our identities' (2005: 241).

The drawing on stories and the emphasis on intimacy in this book have been part of its argument that this is appropriate and illuminating because the concepts of the rural, community and ethnicity are ones that are emotional. The biographic and autobiographic sources and the project's data that have been discussed and examined here all reflect this. The anxious, 'age of grief' arguments put forward by Roger Scruton, Paul Kingsnorth, Roger Askwith, Richard Benson (as well as others long before them George Sturt, Stanley Baldwin, G.K. Chesterton, J.B. Priestley) are intensely emotionally constituted. In some ways what I would suggest is that there is a need to engage with the optics of intimacy and emotions within rural studies – to a much greater extent than has (with a few exceptions) been done (Davidson, Bondi and Smith, 2003). Rural spaces, I have argued through this book, are spaces of emotion.

In this concluding chapter my intention is to recursively return and review some of the threads, including intimacy, that have run through the previous discussions. At its heart this chapter is concerned with an examination of the liminality of rural spaces and the ways in which they are subject to constantly competing demands and interpretations and social struggles. The chapter is structured around the argument that we can organise the contentions and turbulence of rurality, albeit rather roughly and readily, into three key knots to deliberate: ontological insecurity, social exclusion and transformative possibilities. It is to the first of these I now turn.

Rural Spaces, the English Countryside and Ontological Insecurity

One of the contentions of this book is the impossibility of separating and attempting to distinctly bound urban and the rural spaces. Worries and anxieties about events, changes, processes and practices in rural spaces and the countryside are but aspects of worries and anxieties about events, changes, processes and practices in urban spaces.

This is a point made by Michael Woods when he argues that '"rural politics" cannot be defined as politics that occur within rural space but that a politics of the rural transcends rural and urban space enrolling actors in diverse locations and at a range of scales' (2005: 20). It is possible to see this transcendence of rural/urban binaries in a number of the focus group interview conversations – whether it is worries about local social change, crime and safety; about socialness, looking after neighbours and civic engagement or about legislation and over regulation that have already been cited in the previous chapters and in Chapters 5 and 7 in particular. And it is there of course in the unease and contentions as to the relationship between rural space and national identity. As Raymond Williams puts it 'the country and city are changing historical realities, both in themselves and in their inter-relations. Moreover in our own world they represent only two kinds of settlement. Our real social experience is not only of the country and the city, in their most singular forms, but many kinds of intermediate and new kinds of social and physical organisation. Yet the ideas and the images of country and city retain their great force [...] clearly the contrast of city and country is one of the major forms in which we become conscious of a central part of our experience and the crises of our society' (1975: 347). There is certainly something of this idea of a crisis going on in the current literature on the countryside and Englishness which Chapters 1 and 2 discussed. This is framed as a crisis in national identity and this is closely related to a crisis in rural identities and practices or 'ways of life'. We have seen that this is not a new relationality. Stanley Baldwin's fears about the loss of pastoral England sound very similar to the 1930s and 1940s writers that Patrick Wright (1984) examines, who themselves sound very similar to the current 'state of the rural – state of Englishness' commentators. Take for example the *Independent* newspaper's (9 September 2005) coverage of the Campaign for the Protection of Rural England report written by Paul Kingsnorth:

> Creeping urbanisation and development may lead to the destruction of the traditional English countryside in a single generation a report warns today. The remorseless expansion of housing, industry, traffic, road-building and airport construction combined with the steady decline in traditional farming, may mean the treasured, traditional countryside will have all but disappeared by 2035 says the campaign to Protect Rural England [...] In three decades, the report suggests: 'By accident rather than design, much of England has become an anywhere-place, unloved and unloving, a homogenous exurbia, in which everywhere looks the same as everywhere else.'

And compare that with the following extract taken from J.B. Priestley's account of the problems facing rural England at the end of the 1930s written in his essay 'Britain is in Danger',

> Our twentieth century spoiling [of the countryside] [...] has been much worse [than 19th century industrialisation] because instead of concentrating the nasty attack on a few districts, it has set to work to ruin the look of the whole island. Then you could escape from the nasty mess we were making of our country. Now there is hardly any escape. Everywhere you go you notice the same carelessness and nastiness and stupidity. The fairy-tale place has almost gone, only bits of it surviving to remind us, to reproach us [...] Now more and more of this island is being turned into this half and half, neither town nor country and if we do not stop it we shall soon say good-bye for ever to the lovely country our forefathers knew. (1939: 165–6)

Kingsnorth and Priestley could be holding up mirrors to the other despite their writing being 64 years apart. This is the point that others (Williams, 1975 for example) have made – that discourses of cultural loss and irrevocable change are constantly being in and are part of formations of identity. Within narratives of Englishness the rural spaces of the nation get particularly summoned as sites of anxiousness but at the same time they are also required to work affectively as a site of reassurance. In the interconnected, global, late modern, early 21st century it is rural spaces that offer ever enticing ways in which to see and experience what we imagine to be the antithesis of the precarious, uncertain, fearful, in flux, grand scale, individualised social worlds and urban environments in which most people live whether in the cities of the affluent global north or in the megacities of the poor global south (Davis, 2005).

Let's return to Jock Young and his reminder that the 'condition of late modernity is a […] situation where narrative is plagued with doubts, insecurities and a sense of vertigo' (2007: 205). These arguments about the insecurities of late modernity or contemporary capitalism 'where the chaos of reward generates feelings of inchoate unfairness, where success is likely to be transient and inadequately rewarded while failure is readily individualised' (Young, ibid.) were discussed in Chapter 3 in relation to the continuing appeal of community but they can be extended to the rural more specifically. When Zygmunt Bauman (2001: 144) argues that 'we miss community because we miss security, a quality crucial to a happy life, but one which the world we inhabit is ever less able to offer and ever more reluctant to promise' it is possible to see rural spaces working as a spatialised expression of the same social needs to which the idea of community appears to be able to respond. There was something of this convergence taking place in the discussions in Chapter 5 when I examined the extent to which participants in the research were engaged in community making labour. This was driven not by a notion of community *per se* but more by the notion of what was imagined to be happening – or should be happening – within *rural* communities. The anxieties about rural change and new types of countryside are anxieties not only about what anchors national identity in multi-ethnic, globally located, internationally aligned, nationally devolved societies such as the UK but perhaps a deeper emotional attachment and sense of loss – what exactly is there left if the imagined landscapes of rurality and the social relations that go with those disappear altogether from view?

Williams argues that the countryside (although he makes the point that urban backstreets also work in this way) is often associated with childhood and of an ideal and 'idea of childhood'. And by extension this association of particular geographies with childhoods means that they are inflected by this sense of loss and nostalgia. My own recollections in Chapter 5 of the freedoms of growing up in the Pennines and West Wales are part of this process and seem to me now as dreamily idyllic (although the idea of empty and left to ruin farms that we played in as children seems unimaginable in the contemporary gentrified, commodified, post-productive English countryside). But there is an association between the countryside and memory and freedom and safety which both Valentine (2000) and Jones (1997) have examined (see Chapter 7). There is something of this captured for example in J.B. Priestley's account of what a day out in country was like when his mother, father or older sister asked,

Well, what was it like? If it was a good day, there is in your mind a sort of terrific shining jumble, and you try to find words to explain that jumble – the excitement of starting out, the light on the field, the winking of bright water in the streams, the splashing in the pools, the taste of the sandwiches, the green Robin Hood shadows deep in the woods, the smell of grass, the nice tiredness of evening – and so on and so on and so on. It is an exciting but rather desperate business, this trying to explain what it was like. (1939: xii–xiii)

Similarly it is no coincidence that *Country Living* magazine's 'Bring Back the Nature Table' Campaign is all about a rejection of later modernity and 'reconnecting our children with the natural environment' and arguing that 'We all like to see children romping on the grass, collecting leaves and pebbles, patting animals, playing Pooh-sticks. We think of nature as recreational, calming, an *antidote to screen time and shopping centres.* [...] building dens, damming streams and playing in green spaces encourages invention and problem solving' (2008: 54–5. Emphasis added). For Williams all this memory is about structures of feeling in which the adult experience of separation, change, distance, alienation, and about moving to 'modes of using and consuming rather than accepting and enjoying people and things' (1975: 358).

It is within this context of loss and change that rural spaces become a potent pre- and post-modern shorthand for security and timelessness. As the chapters of this book have illustrated this shorthand is able to work effectively and in interconnected ways in both individual and collective identity narratives. Part of this effectiveness is embedded within – and requires – processes in which notions of community and ethnicity are being continually folded. Integral to the arguments as to the uncertainties, fragmentations and senses of precarious that constitute the core features of late modernity is the suggestion that this produces defensive forms of social retreat and regulation. In a world where populations are increasingly required to fend and manage for themselves, where it is peoples' own resources and the market that are relied on rather than the governments and states commentators such as Young (1999; 2007); Bauman (2000; 2001); Garland (2001); Waquant (2002) have argued that western societies have become more entrenched, punitive and exclusive and less public, less civic, less tolerant of difference, rule breaking, transgression and dissent. There is an emphasis on the extremes of social organisation – on control, legislation, punishment, imprisonment, cultural recognition, sameness and closed boundaries, essentialised identities. If English rural spaces get filtered through these arguments it is possible to see the ways in which the anxieties of late modernity can be mapped onto and materially effect what happens in countrysides and it is this which I now examine.

Rural Spaces, the English Countryside, Securitisation and Social Exclusion

As ontological insecurity – and the search for ontological security – intensifies then certain spaces and discourses become particularly asserted, valorised and defended as representing the sought after site of security and reassurance. There are two ways in which I would suggest that this ontological insecurity and the search for ways in which to effectively manage it manifest themselves. The first is through worries about security and safety and the everyday social *practices* that these give rise to. Chapter 6 examined some of these when it spoke of 'panopticon villages' and the surveillance of the neighbourly gaze. Certainly senses of fear and perceptions about a break down in social order and a rise in crime and the inability of the police and/or governments to make effective interventions regularly emerged in the focus group interview conversations. The following extracts evidence some of this. The first two are both examples of the everyday but *multidimensionally* constituted fears and senses of risk:

> Judy: Security is the biggest thing you get in the countryside I think. Looking at different places, I mean well the nearer you get to a place like London, even if you're in a village, you certainly don't have security […] There's no way that you can allow your front door to remain open. You have to follow your children everywhere. Now that might start to apply to this area as well.
>
> Liz: But I would say that it has because our house has been broken into.
>
> Researcher: Do you think something has changed around here then?
>
> Jean: Well you do see a criminal element from areas like Newcastle/
>
> Annette: And because they're mobile, they can move anywhere… (Little Buckley, Northumberland)
>
>
> Annie: Well you wouldn't let a young child out on a pony on this road. The traffic's too bad. She's end up under the wheels and also she might get molested.
>
> […]
>
> Margaret: You were safe to walk in the village weren't you years ago? You never had crime in the village. You never though – when we were children we walked to school and we never thought of being – you never thought there'd be a murder would you? You'd never heard of such a thing. (Farleigh WI)

For the participants in both these conversations the theme of an increased vulnerability and threats predominate and are both personal and social. They range from urban dangers coming into the countryside to children, traffic, child abuse and violent crime. There is a heightened sense that, while being in the countryside does provide some security, this is fragile, uncertain and liable to become less so as threats intrude. The next example focuses more explicitly on making responses to these perceptions of risk and everyday practices of securitisation:

Ricky: We now lock absolutely everything up. We've got a secure gate at the bottom of the farm drive because we used to get people drive up when there was nothing around and they'd try and nick something [...] but we're mostly becoming prisoners in the countryside. I mean it may sound a bit over the top but everyone around us has had to put a security gate up to just keep people out. All the fields we've had to put gates on every one and block all the gaps so nobody can get in basically.

[...]

Jamie: It all comes down to the same thing like that Tony Martin bloke was defending himself on his farm. If they didn't break in they wouldn't have got shot would they? And that's the way it works around here.

Sheena: There was a policeman in the village but they're in the towns now aren't they.

Ricky: I was in the field and I got threatened by three gypsies and I rang the police and he said 'I'm afraid there's nobody around to come and see you'. An hour and a half later the police come round. And I could have been, well, I could have been in a ditch. (Swimbridge YFC)

It is possible to see social retreat here as Ricky describes rural residents – and particularly landowners – taking often dramatic steps to protect property and land. This is not to belittle the senses of anxiety and beleaguerment that are present in this extract but more to connect the ways in which everyday perceptions of crime and vulnerability and being reliant on individualised resources resonates with the penalising privatising discourses that commentators such as David Garland (2001) have argued are shaping and affecting contemporary social relations. The reference that Jamie makes to Tony Martin the Norfolk farmer who was convicted and imprisoned in 2000 for shooting two young burglars who broke into his farm and killing one of them (Martin was released in 2003 after his case was reviewed with a high profile media campaign in support of him) not only takes us back to the anti-regulatory arguments ('that's the way it works round here') that were examined in Chapter 6 but also raises the spectres of those undesirable figures within rural spaces. As we have seen in the examination above the countryside seems to offer spaces of everyday security and safety in an insecure world – albeit seemingly constantly compromised – but that is achieved not only through everyday practices and discourses of reassurance and anxiety but works as imagined and representational spaces of nation and ethnicity too.

From the work that has been done within rural and cultural studies it is clear that English rural spaces have been mobilised in this way as purified spaces of Englishness, the nation and its identity. As Chapter 2 explored, this purification takes the forms of exclusion, othering, marginalisation and denial of those whose presence in rural spaces appears to disrupt or represent a threat to authenticity of rural spaces working as Englishness. As David Sibley puts it 'dominant rural communities in England have at different times identified threatening, abject others in the form of colonial and ex-colonial peoples, nomads, the urban working class and youth cultures. They have all defiled rural space; they have all come from somewhere else' (1995: 220).

In particular it has been the whitening of English rurality that has drawn commentary and there is now an extensive body of mainly small scale, qualitative oriented research which documents and charts the widespread experiences of racism and racialised exclusions within rural areas. The various policy and rural agencies' uncertainties as to how to respond to this, and to the notion of multicultural, multiethnic populations existing in the UK outside the traditional metropolitan centres, remain. This racism may take explicitly hostile and violent forms (see Chakraborti and Garland, 2004 for example) or it may work in more insidious and incremental ways. For example Katherine Tyler's research in Greenville a villagey suburb of Leicester found that the white middle class village residents tended to speak of how affluent South Asian village residents chose not be part of the community and isolated themselves because they did not join in the activities and neighbourly networks which acted to continually confirm the idea of Greenville as a caring village. As Tyler notes although wealthy South Asian residents had 'acquired the material trappings of an affluent middle-class lifestyle' for white residents 'they were thought to lack the "cultural ingredients"' (Ortner, 2002: 12) that constitute the appropriate ways of behaving in Greenville's imagined 'village' community' (2006: 136). Tyler cites the work of Malory Nye (2001) who found very similar patterns of white middle class racialised unease in relation to his research on the relationship between Britain and Hinduism. Interviewing an Asian Hindu resident in an affluent Oxfordshire village Nye was told that while the surrounding white neighbours were pleasant and friendly they had also complained to the council about the noise and smells associated with this resident using the Hindu temple in his garden for religious festivals despite the acceptance of garden parties held by white middle class residents. The findings of Tyler and Nye resonate with the findings made in Chapter 5 about the continual conditionality of social inclusion in the English countryside (see also Neal and Agyeman, 2006 and Garland and Chakraborti, 2007). This demand for sameness and 'fitting in' represents a discursive attempt to flatten out rural heterogeneity and so maintain dominant constructions of 'recognisable' and community organised rural social relations. Hetherington (2006: 182) makes a similar point when he notes that New Age Traveller readings of rural landscapes are 'at odds' with dominant interpretations of those same spaces and which see such counter figures as having 'no part' in them. The imperative to remove them from those landscapes involved, in the case of New Age Travellers, a whole series of agencies from central government to local authorities to the police and bodies like the National Trust and English Heritage.

In part these purifying responses reflect the demands of the re-populated rural and counterurbanisation movements which have invested emotionally and financially in a particularly fantasised and material countryside (Woods, 2005: 17; Chapter 2) and in part they reflect the search for, and efforts to establish, security through the rejection – or at least the problematisation – of cultural and social difference. But perhaps more than anything my concern here has been to emphasise how securing the countryside, ethnicity and community is an ongoing, always unfinished, laborious, emotional and contradictory project. It is this final theme that I now consider.

Rural Spaces and the Transformative Possibilities of Community, Ethnicity and the English Countryside

I have argued across the previous chapters that countryside, community and ethnicity are concepts that are each in a relational, contested and continuing ascendancy. Their durability (as in the case of community and the countryside) and their emergent rise (as in the case of ethnicity) can be analytically located in anxieties 'from above' about the nation/al, its narratives and the meanings and interpretations of Englishness in a multi-ethnic, multicultural, devolving UK. These 'from above' anxieties are also filtered through the turbulences, contentions and uncertainties of the ever in-flux, local–global world. In this context it means that as Chapter 3 and a range of commentators (see Taylor, 2003; Day, 2006; Mooney and Neal, 2009 for example) have noted we are likely to see ever more of 'community' in populist, political and policy discourses. This is because community has rather unique latitude in that it can work very effectively as a fantasy, as a desired imaginary, as a site of social and emotional resource, as a discourse of connection and care, as well as a site of defensive and exclusion. It offers a site in which individual and collective narratives of belonging can be read. Perhaps community's core seduction and anomaly is that it appears to be able to work at a beyond social divisions scale as well as concretising social divisions. We saw some of this strange duality in Howard Newby's research in East Anglia where he argued there were two communities – the 'dark' or marginal community of poorer, agricultural workers and the 'whole' village community which nevertheless spoke of an inclusive belonging and was able to manage diversity of class and include within its boundary both poor and affluent village residents.

There is a similarity to community in the labile, inclusive *and* defensive, personal and public nature of ethnicity. Chapter 4 discussed in detail the ways in which ethnicity has rapidly moved from its anthropological contexts and usage into widespread everyday and political usage as populations variously – and at times violently – claim, reject and ascribe ethnic identities. However, ethnicity does not quite work as a condensation symbol in the same easy way as community and the countryside. Its populist, policy and political use as a description of, and something belonging to, the other, the unfamiliar and of cultural difference mean that its associations are not straightforwardly or overwhelmingly warm and 'good'.

The ways in which ethnicity can work as a form of individual and collective identification, as descriptor for 'ways of life', as a component of nation/ality, as a narrative of sameness and belonging as well as a narrative of difference and separateness, means that discourses of ethnicity are likely to be durable. Ethnicity is a concept which is inflects and reflects community.

This book has been about an examination as to why ethnicity inflects and reflects rurality. The concepts of the countryside and rurality sit comfortably alongside community and ethnicity. Chapter 2 described the ways in which the rural and the countryside have been reconceptualised as culturally as much as – more than? – geographically located. As Cloke and Thrift (1994: 1) have asserted 'the meanings and intensities of the rural have multiplied [...] It is now an infinitely more mobile and malleable term'. It is this mobility that is now associated with the concept of the rural that lends rurality the same 'qualities' as those possessed by the categories of community and ethnicity. In other words the diversity in the ways that the rural can work and the multidimensionality of what it means and how it is mobilised, desired and consumed means that it constantly challenges and unsettles any singular interpretation. The contested heart of each of these concepts is a reflected in the different and diverse ways in which purchases may be made on them from above and, importantly, also *from below*. In other words while community, ethnicity and rurality have a social and cultural architecture and are enacted and realised through social practices they not only have a materiality but are invested in ways of making sense of individual and collective experiences and perceptions. The ability of these concepts to do this is reflected in the ways in which the specificity and distinctiveness of rural place at a county level, i.e. between Hertfordshire, North Devon and Northumberland, was not significant. The 'countryside of the mind', the immediate locale and the national imaginary were what preoccupied and bundled together the ways in which participants spoke of rural spaces. The concepts of community, ethnicity and rurality each share also a pre-modern materiality (as Chapters 3 and 4 examined) which has a post-modern appeal in the context of the uncertainties and insecurities of late modernity.

I want to think through 'from below' for a minute longer. I began in Chapter 1 by describing the research project from which much of the empirical data used in this book has been drawn, as involving participants who could rather broadly be defined as not representative of rural populations but were a sample of those rural populations who are easily accounted for and/or included within mainstream and dominant rural narratives. Noting the concerns expressed by Murdoch and Pratt (1992) and also Cloke and Little (1997) about the need to not let a concern with describing and visibilising rural marginality and otherness lead to a 'research tourism' in which the others studied became just that – objects of academic interest – this project drew on the postcolonial notion of otherness which is an argument that the defining of others is at the same time a definition of the centre. In this way the use meant that the project and its research intentions did not lose sight of the processes of power and powerlessness with social relations. In short by focussing on the 'mainstream' and the 'ordinary' there was an opportunity to listen to and examine what the experiences and everyday processes of being accounted for, of inclusion and of belonging were and to describe what these look like and hear about how they are lived.

Seen through the optics of community and ethnicity and rurality Chapters 5, 6 and 7 showed how these processes appear as fragile, elusive, contradictory and insecure. They were framed by anxiety, in need of constant sustenance and maintenance. For example Chapter 5 examined how community and connection were enacted within rural spaces which created sociality, networks of care and conviviality but not only did this enactment require intensive labour it involved a conscious intent to make structures of community feeling. In this way the chapter suggested that the organised enactment of rural community skirted close to and/or slipped into technicism and strategies of governance and control even as they could be understood as practices of mutuality and conviviality (see also Mosely and Phal, 2005). The multidimensionality and contradictory interpretations of rural spaces were the concern of Chapter 6. It showed that participants were able to move from embracing the watchful, knowing and regulatory gaze to desiring isolation, from sociality to equating rural spaces with freedom and counter regulatory values. The chapter argued that this absence of consensus within mainstream discourses as to the meaning of countrysides illuminates the fragmented and unsettled ways in which rurality can diversely animate social relations, emotions and practices. In Chapter 1 I drew on Michael Bell's arguments about the importance of scrutinising the social experience of nature for understanding the rural-nation identities. This emerged as a core feature of Chapter 3's discussion of ethnicity and was picked up again, along with the idea of the animating possibilities and multidimensionality of non-human things in shaping social discourses and practices, in Chapter 7. Central to this chapter were the ways in which participants looked to and engaged with rural nature as the key referent for explaining their senses of attachment and affection for their surrounds and locality. While this enrolment of the nature–culture relation was extended to ways of describing and defining Englishness this was an elusive – but nevertheless effective – process. Both of these points are core to my suggestion that placing an emphasis on nature–culture hybridities offers a way to understand the apparent contradiction of this elusive but effective couplet. Drawing on and mobilizing non-human entities such as weather, seasons, fields, types of light, greenness, trees within ethnic formations is unlikely to secure and settle them. Rural nature becomes in these processes all about the corporeal – the senses, the emotions, and the body – as the data cited in earlier chapters evidenced. The residents in Bell's Childerley study spoke in very similar terms to those in the focus group conversations. For example Bell quotes a farmer explaining his embodied affinity to the countryside,

> *It's a sensuous thing almost.* The beauty in the countryside is something too, just
> walking around in the autumn in the mist. Once your eyes have been opened to
> beauty you can see it everywhere [...] – the trees, the sky, the ever changing sky,
> cattle and sheep. That's all very, very satisfying. It's part of the privilege really
> and enjoyment of living in the country. (1994: 91. Emphasis added)

Of course the corporeal aspect of the inter-relationship between the person and
rural nature does not mean that its extension to a national frame leaves it unable to
work in powerful ways. In some ways it is because it *is* so elusive and slight it that
it works to summon up and assemble an immediately recognisable Englishness.
This brings me back to Michael Billig's arguments that it is through the familiar
and the banal that ideas of nation – particularly dominant national identities – have
to be located and are routinely flagged because 'nationhood is near the surface of
contemporary life' (1995: 93). Indeed Billig notes that the weather – as it is daily
reported on in the news – acts as powerful site for the daily reminder of nation
and home 'the weather – with its "other places", its "elsewheres" and its "around
the country's" – must have its deictic centre within the homeland. "The weather"
appears as an objective, physical category, yet it is contained within the national
boundaries' (ibid.: 117).

So my argument here is not that the ephemeral and corporeal architectures of
Englishness leave the boundaries of ethnic identification insecure and open but rather
that, as ANT emphasises, nature and non-human things are not simply compliant
and biddable instruments or sites to be enrolled and deployed by ontological
and political practices in efforts to secure identities and claim making and assert
entitlement and belonging within contested social worlds. Like the concepts of
community and ethnicity, rural nature and non-human things are unpredictable
and their inter-relational agency with humans may lead to unpredictable outcomes
and possibilities. As Hinchliffe argues, 'Nature doesn't seem to be working as a
rallying site for everyone and everything anymore. If in the past it has allowed
us to terminate debate and – like God before it – secure an agreeable collective,
things certainly don't seem to be as easy now. Already faced with an unruly and
heterogeneous populace, a massive demographic of humans and non-humans who
won't fall into place (Callon and Latour, 1994), what or who counts is very much
up for grabs.' (2007: 188).

This book has suggested that in this openness there are increasing possibilities
for re-interpretation and for the creation and establishment of more diverse
emotional and political affinities and attachments to rural spaces. In putting an
emphasis on the urgency of filtering identity and ethnicity through nature and the
non-human I have tried to suggest that we not only recognise the ontological and
political work that gets done through nature–social crossings and its exclusionary
and punitive dimensions, but also recognises the inclusionary and transformative
possibilities of nature–social crossings for ethnic identity formations. Sociology –

with its modernist focus on the social – has been rather cautious in its willingness to (re)engage with the natural and the notions of non-human and human inter-relational agency. This is understandable given the instrumentalist and insidious ways in which the natural has been enrolled in the legitimation, and as the explanation, of social divisions and processes of subjugation to say nothing of its reinforcing of common sense thinking. It is, nevertheless a reticence which leaves some of the contemporary categories of the social unaccounted for.

This is the argument made by theorists such as Nikolas Rose (2007) when he suggests that the relationship between biology and sociology is shifting and is now in need of reappraisal and Steve Fuller (2006) who urges sociologists to 'pay attention to biology' and David Skinner (2007) who suggests there is an increasing 'interplay' between natural and social science that requires sociological recognition. According to Skinner there is cultural content to life science and common ground in terms of 'wrestling with shared practical, methodological, epistemological and political problems' (2007: 940). The idea of a dialogue and exchange between and across once firmly demarcated academic disciplines is of course an integral feature of ANT approaches with their emphasis on the connectivities and combining relations between science, technologies, humans, machines and other non-human things. While this book has been about nature and rural spaces and identifications, it has argued that the urban is not separate from this. The relationship between the non-human and urban spaces and processes of identification and belonging is as pertinent and pronounced. As Nigel Thrift puts it in his discussions of speed, light and mobility, in a 'cyborg culture in which the boundaries between humans and machines have become ever more permeable, leading to more and more actant subjects and an increasing emphasis on machinic metaphors and practices [...] it seems to me to be important to recognise this state of affairs and work with it' (1994: 235).

But I do not want to finish with cyborgs. I want to finish with Richard Mabey's cat. Mabey uses his beloved cat Blackie as a metaphor for the ability to continually negotiate and inhabit the cross-over and inter-relational sites and practices of the natural and the social – 'cats' writes Mabey (2007: 226) 'seem to me to be messengers. Their effortless passing between the wild and domestic suggests the kind of grace we need as a species to move between nature and culture'. And in some ways, social science approaches to understanding the defensive, enclosed, emotional, open and transformative aspects of ethnic formations, nation, ontological and political identity, rural space and practices of social inclusion and attachment will be enhanced if our analysis can imitate Mabey's cat and work through, within and across human and non-human combinations and connections.

Bibliography

Agyeman, J. 1989. Black People in a White Landscape: Social and Environmental Justice, *Built Environment*, Vol. 16 (3) pp 232–6.

Agyeman, J. and Spooner, R. 1997. Ethnicity and the Rural Environment, in *Contested Countryside Cultures: Otherness, Marginalization and Rurality* edited by P. Cloke and J. Little. London: Routledge.

Ahmed, S. 2000. *Strange Encounters: Embodied Otherness in Post-Coloniality*. London: Routledge.

Alleyne, B. 2002. An idea of community and its discontents: towards a more reflexive sense of belonging in multicultural Britain, *Ethnic and Racial Studies*, Vol. 25, No.4, 607–27.

Amit, V. and Rapport, N. 2002. *The Trouble with Community: Anthropological Reflections on Movement, Identity and Collectivity*. London: Pluto Press.

Anderson, B. 1991. *Imagined Communities*. London: Verso.

Andrews, M. 1997. *The Acceptable Face of Feminism: The Women's Institute as a Social Movement*. London: Lawrence and Wishart.

Anthias, F. and Yuval-Davis, N. 1992. *Racialised Boundaries: Race, Nation, Gender, Colour and Class in the Anti-racist Struggle*. London: Routledge.

Arensberg, C. and Kimball, S. 1940. *Family and Community in Ireland* 2nd Edition 1968. Oxford: Oxford University Press.

Ashcroft, B., Griffiths, G. and Tiffin, H. 1998. *Post-colonial Studies: The Key Concepts*. London: Routledge.

Askins, K. 2004. *Visible Communities' Use and Perceptions of the Peak District and North York National Parks*. Preliminary Report to the National Park Trust and Economic and Social Research Council.

Askins, K. 2006. New Countryside? New country: visible communities in the English national parks in *The New Countryside? Ethnicity, Nation and Exclusion in Contemporary Rural Britain* edited by S. Neal and J. Agyeman. Bristol: The Policy Press.

Askwith, R. 2007. *The Lost Village: In Search of a Forgotten Rural England*. London: Ebury Press.

Back, L. 1996. *New Ethnicities and Urban Culture*. London: University College Press.

Back, L. 2007. *The Art of Listening*. Oxford: Berg.

Balibar, E. 1991. *The Nation Form in Race, Nation, Class* edited by E. Balibar and I. Wallerstien. London: Verso.

Banton, M. 1983. *Racial and Ethnic Competition*. Cambridge: Cambridge University Press.

Banton, M. 1987. *Racial Theories*. Cambridge: Cambridge University Press.

Barth, F. 1969. *Ethnic Groups and Boundaries*. Boston: Little Brown.

Bauman, Z. 2001. *Community: Seeking Security in an Insecure World*. Cambridge: Polity.

Beck, U. 2000. *What is Globilization?* Cambridge: Polity.

Beck, U. 2002. The cosmopolitan society and its enemies, *Theory, Culture and Society*, Vol 19: 17–44.

Bell, C. and Newby, H. 1971. *Community Studies*. London: Allan and Unwin.

Bell, D. 1997. Anti-Idyll: Rural Horror in *Contested Countryside Cultures* edited by P. Cloke and J. Little. London: Routledge.

Bell, M. 1994. *Childerley: Nature and Morality in a Country Village*. Chicago: University of Chicago Press.

Benson, R. 2005. *The Farm*. London: Hamish Hamilton.

Bhabha, H. 1990. *Nation and Narration*. London: Routledge.

Bhattacharyya, G. 1999. Teaching race in cultural studies: a ten-step programme of personal development in *Ethnic and Racial Studies Today* edited by M. Bulmer and J. Solomos. London: Routledge.

Billig, M. 2002. *Banal Nationalism*. London: Sage.

Blythe, R. 1969. *Akenfield*. Middlesex: Penguin.

Bondi, L., Davidson, J. and Smith, M. 2005. Geography's 'Emotional Turn' in *Emotional Geographies* edited by J. Davidson, L. Bondi and M. Smith. Aldershot: Ashgate.

Brah, A. 1996. *Cartographies of Diaspora: Contesting Identities*. London: Routledge.

Bunce, M. 1994. *The Countryside Ideal*. London: Routledge.

Bunce, M. 2003. Reproducing rural idylls in *Country Visions* edited by P. Cloke. Essex: Pearson Education Prentice Hall.

Callon, M. 1999. Some Elements of a Sociology of Translation: Domestication of the Scallops and the Fishermen of Saint Brieuc Bay in *The Science Studies Reader* edited by M. Biagioli. London: Routledge: 67–83.

Chakraborti, N. and Garland, J. 2004. *Rural Racism*. Devon: Willan.

Chavez, S. 2005. Community, ethnicity and class in a changing rural California town, *Rural Sociology*, 70, 3, 28–49.

Clarke, J. 2006. Fantasies of community and community as governance. Paper presented to ESRC Policing in an Age of Diversity seminar, University of Leicester.

Clarke, J. 2009. People and places: the search for community in *Community: Welfare, Crime and Society* edited by G. Mooney and S. Neal. Maidenhead: Open University Press McGraw Hill.

Clifford, J. 1986. Introduction: Partial Truths in *Writing Culture* edited by J. Clifford and G. Marcus. Berkley: University of California Press.

Cloke, P. 1994. (En)culturing Political Economy: A Day in the Life of a 'Rural Geographer' in *Writing the Rural* edited by P. Cloke, M. Doel, D. Matless, M. Phillips and N. Thrift. London: Paul Chapman Publishing.

Cloke, P. 1997a. Country backwater to virtual village? Rural studies and the cultural turn, *Journal of Rural Studies*, 13, 4, 367–76.

Cloke, P. 1997b. Marginality, poverty and rurality in *Contested Countryside Cultures* edited by P. Cloke and J. Little. London: Routledge.

Cloke, P. (ed.) 2003. *Country Visions*. Harlow: Essex: Prentice Hall.

Cloke, P. 2004. Rurality and racialising others: Out of place in the countryside? in *Rural Racism* edited by N. Chakraborti and J. Garland. Devon: Willan.

Cloke, P. and Jones, O. 2002. *Tree Cultures: The Place of Trees and Trees in their Place*. London: Berg.

Cloke, P. and Little, J. (eds) 1997. *Contested Countryside Cultures: Otherness, Marginalization and Rurality*. London: Routledge.

Cloke, P. and Thrift, N. 1994. Refiguring the 'Rural' in *Writing the Rural: Five Cultural Geographies* edited by P. Cloke, M. Doel, D. Matless, M. Phillips and N. Thrift. London: Paul Chapman Publishing.

Cochrane, A. and Newman, J. 2009. Community and policy making in *Community: Welfare, Crime and Society* edited by G. Mooney and S. Neal. Maidenhead: Open University Press McGraw Hill.

Cochrane, A. and Talbot, D. (eds) 2008. *Security: Welfare, Crime and Society*. Maidenhead: Open University Press McGraw Hill.

Cohen, A. 1985. *The Symbolic Construction of Community*. London: Routledge.

Cohen, A.P. 1982. *Belonging, Identity and Social Organisation in British Rural Cultures*. Manchester: Manchester University Press.

Cohen, A.P. 1982. Blockade: a case study of local consciousness in an extra-local event in *Belonging: Identity and Social Organisation in British Rural Cultures* edited by A.P. Cohen. Manchester: Manchester University Press.

Connolly, P. 2006. 'It goes without saying (well, sometimes)': Racism, Whiteness and Identity in Northern Ireland in *The New Countryside? Ethnicity, Nation and Exclusion in Contemporary Rural Britain* edited by S. Neal and J. Agyeman. Bristol: The Policy Press.

Cresswell, T. 1996. *In Place/Out of Place: Geography, Ideology and Transgression*. Minneapolis: University of Minnesota Press.

Crow, G. and Allan, G. 1994. *Community Life*. London: Harvester Wheatsheaf.

Darby, W. 2000. *Landscape and Identity: Geographies of Nation and Class in England*. Oxford: Berg.

Davidson, L., Bondi, L. and Smith, M. 2005. *Emotional Geographies*. Aldershot: Ashgate.

Davis, M. 2006. *Planet of Slums*. London: Verso.

Day, G. 2006. *Community and Everyday Life*. London: Routledge.

De Lima, P. 2001. *Needs Not Numbers: An Exploration of Minority Ethnic Communities in Scotland*. London: Commission for Racial Equality.

Derbyshire, H. 1994. *Not in Norfolk: Tackling the Invisibility of Racism*. London: Commission for Racial Equality.

Dhalech, M. 1999. *Challenging the Rural Idyll: The Final Report of the Rural Racial Equality Project*. London: NACAB.

Edelman, M. 1977. *Political Language: Words that Succeed and Policies that Fail*. New York: Academic Press.

Edwards, R. 1990. Connecting Method and Epistemology: A White Woman Interviewing Black Women, *Women's Studies International Forum*, 13, 477–90.

Etzioni, A. 1995. *The Spirit of Community*. London: Fontana Press.

Eyles, J. 1985. *Senses of Place*. Cheshire: Silverbrook Press.

Farquhar, C. 1999. Are focus groups suitable for 'sensitive' topics? in *Developing Focus Group Research* edited by R. Barbour and J. Kitzinger. Sage: London.

Fenton, S. 1999. *Ethnicity, Racism, Class and Culture*. London: Macmillan.

Fine, M. 1994. Working the Hyphens: Reinventing Self and Other in Qualitative Research in *The Handbook of Qualitative Research* edited by N. Denzin and Y. Lincoln. Sage: London.

Forster, E.M. 2000. *Howard's End*. London: Penguin.

Foucault, M. 1979. *Discipline and Punish*. Harmondsworth: Penguin.

Foucault, M. 1980. *Power/Knowledge*. Brighton: Harvester.

Foucault, M. 1986. Of Other Spaces, *Diacritics*, 16(1), 22–7.

Frankenberg, R. 1993. *The Social Construction of Whiteness*. London: Routledge.

Fuller, S. 2006. *The New Sociological Imagination*. London: Sage.

Garland, J. and Chakraborti, N. 2007. Protean Times? Exploring the relationships between policing, community and 'race', *Rural England, Criminology and Criminal Justice*, Vol. 7, No. 4: 347–67.

Geertz, C. 1988. *Works and Lives: The Anthropologist as Author*. Stanford: Stanford University Press.

Gilroy, P. 1987. *There Ain't No Black in the Union Jack*. London: Unwin.

Gilroy, P. 2004. *After Empire, Melancholia or Convivial Culture?* London: Routledge.

Glendinning, A., Nuttall, M., Hendry, L., Kloep, M. and Wood, S. 2003. Rural Communities and well-being: a good place to grow up?, *Sociological Review*, 51, 129–56.

Goffman, E. 1959. *Presentation of Self in Everyday Life*. New York: Anchor Press.

Goffman, E. 1963. *Behaviour in Public Places: Notes on the Social Organisation of Gatherings*. New York: The Free Press.

Goldberg, D. 1993. *Racist Culture: Philosophy and the Politics of Meaning*. Oxford: Blackwell.

Green, J. and Hart, L. 1999. The Impact of Context on Data in *Developing Focus Group Research* edited by R. Barbour and J. Kitzinger. London: London.

Gupta, A. and Ferguson, J. 1997. Culture, power, place: ethnographies at the end of an era in *Culture, Power, Place: Explorations in Critical Anthropology* edited by A. Gupta and J. Ferguson. North Carolina and London: Duke University Press.

Halfacree, K. 1997. Contrasting roles for the post-productivist countryside: a postmodern perspective on counterurbanisation in *Contested Countryside Cultures* edited by P. Cloke and J. Little. London: Routledge.

Halfacree, K. 2007. Trail by space for a 'radical rural': Introducing alternative localities, representations and lives, *Journal of Rural Studies*, 23, Vol 2 125–141.

Hall, S. 1992. The New Ethnicities in *Race, Culture and Difference* edited by J. Donald and A. Rattansi. London: Sage.

Hall, S. 2000. The Multicultural Question in *Un/settled Multiculturalisms: Diasporas, Entanglements, Transruptions* edited by B. Hesse. London: Zed Books.

Halliday, J. and Coombes, M. 1995. In search of counterurbanisation: some evidence from Devon on the relationship between patterns of migration and motivation, *Journal of Rural Studies*, 11, No. 4: 433–46.

Haraway, D. 1991. *Simians, Cyborgs and Women: The Reinvention of Nature*. New York: Routledge, and London: Free Association Books.

Haw, K. 1996. Exploring the Educational Experiences of Muslim Girls: Tales told to Tourists – Should the White Researcher Stay At Home? *British Educational Research Journal*, 22, 319–30.

Hetherington, K. 1997. *The Badlands of Modernity*. London: Routledge.

Hetherington, K. 2000. *New Age Travellers: Vanloads of Uproarious Humanity*. London: Cassells.

Hetherington, K. 2006. Visions of England: New Age Travellers and the idea of ethnicity in *The New Countryside? Ethnicity, Nation and Exclusion in Contemporary Rural Britain* edited by S. Neal and J. Agyeman. Bristol: The Policy Press.

Hinchliffe, S. 2007. *Geographies of Nature: Societies, Environments Ecologies*. London: Sage.

Hobsbawm, E. 1994. *The Age of Extremes*. London: Michel Joseph.

Holloway, S.L. and Valentine, G. 2000. Spatiality and the new social studies of childhood. *Sociology*, 34, 763–83.

Howkins, A. 1986. The discovery of rural England in *Englishness, Politics and Culture 1880–1920* edited by R. Colls and P. Dodd. London: Croom Helm.

Hughes, A. (1997) Women and rurality: gendered experiences of 'community' in village life in *Revealing Rural 'Others'* edited by P. Milbourne, London: Pinter.

Hutchinson, J. and Smith, A.D. 1996. *Ethnicity*. Oxford: Oxford University Press.

Iganski, P. and Levin, J. 2004. Cultures of hate in the urban and the rural: assessing the impact of extremist organisations in *Rural Racism* edited by N. Chakraborti and J. Garland. Devon: Willan.

Jay, E. 1992. *Keep Them in Birmingham*. London: Commission for Racial Equality.

Jenkins, R. 1997. *Rethinking Ethnicity: Arguments and Explorations*. London: Sage.

Jones, O. 1997. Little figures, big shadows: country childhood stories in *Contested Countryside Cultures* edited by P. Cloke and J. Little. London: Routledge.

Kingsnorth, P. 2007. *Real England*. London: Portebello.

Laerke, A. 2003. *Children and Their Adults: Discipline and Bullying in an English Village*. Unpublished PhD thesis: University of London.

Latour, B. 1989. *We have Never Been Modern*. Hertfordshire: Havester Wheatsheaf.

Laurier, E. and Philo, C. 2005. *Cold Shoulders and Napkins Handed: Gestures of Responsibility* (draft). Glasgow: University of Glasgow.

Law, J. (ed.) 1992. *A Sociology of Monsters: Essays on Power, Technology and Domination*. London: Routledge Sociological Review Monograph.

Lefebvre, H. 1991. *The Production of Space*. Oxford: Blackwell.

Mabey, R. 2006. *Nature Cure*. London: Pimlico.

Mac an Ghaill, M. 1999. *Contemporary Racism and Ethnicities: Social and Cultural Transformations*. Buckingham, Open University Press.

MacGregor, S. 2001. The problematic community in *Understanding Social Problems* edited by M. May, E. Brunsden and R. Page. London: Blackwell.

Macnaughten, P. and Urry, J. 2001. *Bodies of Nature*. London: Sage.

Malik, K. 1996. *The Meaning of Race: Race, History and Culture in Western Society*. Basingstoke: Macmillan.

Matless, D. 1994. Doing the English Village, 1945–1990: An Essay in Imaginative Geography in *Writing the Rural* edited by P. Cloke, M. Doel, D. Matless, M. Phillips and N. Thrift. London: Paul Chapman Publishing.

Matless, D. 1998. Taking Pleasure in England: landscape and citizenship in the 1940s in *The Right to Belong: Citizenship and National Identity in Britain, 1930–1990* edited by R. Weight and A. Beach. London: I.B.Taurus.

May, T. 1997. *Social Research, Issues, Methods and Process*, 2nd edition. Buckingham: Open University Press.

Miles, R. 1989. *Racism*. London: Routledge.

Mooney, G. and Neal, S. (eds) 2009. *Community: Welfare, Crime and Society*. Maidenhead: Open University Press McGraw Hill.

Morgan, D.L. 1997. *Focus Groups as Qualitative Research*, 2nd edition. London: Sage.

Moseley, M. and Pahl, R. 2007. *Social Capital in Rural Places*. London: DEFRA.

Murdoch, J. 2003. Co-constructing the countryside: hybrid networks and the extensive self in *Country Visions* edited by P. Cloke. Harlow: Pearson.

Murdoch, J. and Pratt, A. 1994. Rural Studies of power and the power of rural studies: a reply to Philo, *Journal of Rural Studies*, 10, 83–7.

Murdoch, J. and Pratt, A. 1997. From the Power of Topography to the Topography of Power in *Contested Countryside Cultures* edited by P. Cloke and J. Little. London: Routledge.

Neal, S. 1995. Researching Powerful People from Feminist and Anti-Racist Perspectives: A Note on Gender, Collusion and Marginality, *British Educational Research Journal*, 21, 4, 517–31.

Neal, S. 2002. Rural landscapes, representations and racism: examining multicultural citizenship and policy-making in the English countryside, *Ethnic and Racial Studies*, Vol. 25, 3, 442–61.

Neal, S. 2002. Rural landscapes, racism and representation: examining multicultural citizenship and policy-making in *The English Countryside Race and Ethnic Studies*, 25, 3, 442–61.

Neal, S. and Agyeman, J. (eds) 2006. *The New Countryside? Ethnicity, Nation and Exclusion in Contemporary Rural Britain*. Bristol: The Policy Press.

Neal, S. and Agyeman, J. 2006. Remaking English Ruralities: processes of belonging and becoming, continuity and change in racialised spaces in *The New Countryside? Ethnicity, Nation and Exclusion in Contemporary Rural Britain* edited by S. Neal and J. Agyeman. Bristol: The Policy Press.

Neal, S. and Walters, S. 2006. Strangers asking strange questions? A methodological narrative on researching belonging and identity in the English countryside, *Journal of Rural Studies*, Vol. 22, 2, 177–89.

Norris, C. and Armstrong, G. 1999. *The Maximum Surveillance Society: The Rise of CCTV*. Oxford: Berg.

Pahl, R. 1966. The rural–urban continuum, *Sociologica Ruralis*, 6, 320.

Paxman, J. 1998. *The English, A Portrait of a People*. London: Penguin.

Philo, C. 1992. Neglected Rural Geographies: a review, *Journal of Rural Studies*, 8, 193–207.

Priestly, J.B. 1939. *Our Nation's Heritage*. London: Dent and Sons Ltd.

Probyn, E. 1993. *Sexing the Self: Gendered Positions in Cultural Studies*. Routledge: London.

Probyn, E. 1996. *Outside Belongings*. Routledge: London.

Putnam, R. 2000. *Bowling Alone: The Collapse and Revival of American Community*. New York: Simon and Schuster.

Rees, A.D. 1950. *Life in a Welsh Countryside*. Cardiff: University of Wales Press.

Rishbeth, C. 2006. Rwanda in Sheiffield: the global/local distinctiveness of greenspace. Sheffield:University of Sheffiled: http://www.hrionline.ac.uk/matshef/MScopy.htm (accessed July 2007).

Ritzer, G. 2002. *Sociological Theory*. 5th edition. London: McGraw-Hill.

Rose, N. 2007. *The Politics of Life Itself: Biomedicine, Power and Subjectivity in the Twenty-first Century*. Oxford: Princetown University Press.

Said, E. 1978. *Orientalism: Western Concepts of the Orient*. London: Penguin.

Savage, M., Bagnall, G. and Longhurst, B. 2005. *Globalisation and Belonging*. London: Sage.

Scruton, R. 2000. *England: An Elegy*. London: Chatto and Windus.

Short, B. 1992. *The English Rural Community: Image and Analysis*. Cambridge University Press: Cambridge.

Sibley, D. 1995. *Geographies of Exclusion*. London: Routledge.

Sibley, D. 1997. Endangering the Sacred: Nomads, Youth Cultures and the English Countryside in *Contested Countryside Cultures: Otherness, Marginalization and Rurality* edited by P. Cloke and J. Little. London: Routledge.

Simmel, G. 1950. The Stranger in *The Sociology of Georg Simmel*. The Free Press: New York.

Simon, B. 2005. The Return of Panopticism, *Surveillance and Society*, 3, 1: 1–20.

Skinner, D. 2007. Groundhog day? The strange case of sociology, race and 'science', *Sociology*, Vol 41, No 5: 931–44.

Smith, S. 2008. Editorial and Bring Back the Nature Table, *Country Living*, July: 9, 54–5.

Soja, E. 1996. *Thirdspace, Journeys to Los Angeles and other Real-and-Imagined Places*. Oxford: Blackwell.

St. Louis, B. 2003. Sport, genetics and the 'natural athlete': The resurgence of racial science, *Body and Society*, 9, 2, 75–95.

Stacey, M. 1969. The myth of community studies, *British Journal of Sociology*, Vol. 20, 134–47.

Strathern, M. 1982. The village as an idea: constructs of village-ness in Elmdon, Essex in *Belonging: Identity and Social Organisation in British Rural Cultures* edited by A.P. Cohen. Manchester: Manchester University Press.

Thrift, N. 2005. But malice aforethought: cities and the natural history of hatred, *Transaction of the Institute of British Geographers*, 30, 133–50.

Tönnies, F. 1963. *Community and Society*. New York: Harper and Row.

Troyna, B. 1998. The Whites of My Eyes, Nose and Ears: A Reflexive Account of 'Whiteness' in Race-Related Research in *Researching Racism in Education: Politics, Theory and Practice* edited by P. Connolly and B. Troyna. Buckingham: Open University.

Troyna, B. and Carrington, B. 1993. Whose Side are We On? Ethical Dilemmas in Research on Race and Education in *Racism and Education* edited by B. Troyna. Buckingham: Open University.

Tyler, K. 2006. Village people: race, class, nation and the community spirit in *The New Countryside? Ethnicity, Nation and Exclusion in Contemporary Rural Britain* edited by S. Neal and J. Agyeman. Bristol: The Policy Press.

Urry, J. 2002. *The Tourist Gaze*, 2nd edition. London: Sage.

Valentine, G. 1997. A safe place to grow up? Parenting, perceptions of children's safety and the rural idyll, *Journal of Rural Studies,* 13, 137–48.

Wallman, S. 1986. Ethnicity and the boundary process in context in *Theories of Race and Ethnicity* edited by J. Rex and D. Mason. Cambridge: Cambridge University Press.

Walters, S. 2003. *Bangladeshi Pupils: Experiences, Identity and Achievement.* Unpublished PhD thesis: Oxford University.

Ware, V. 2007. *Who Cares about Britishness?* London: Arcadia.

Whatmore, S. 2002. *Hybrid Geographies: Nature, Culture, Spaces*. London: Sage.

Williams, R. 1979. *The Country and the City*. London: Chatto and Windus.

Woods, M. and Goodwin, M. 2003. Applying the rural: governance and policy in rural areas in *Country Visions* edited by P. Cloke. Essex: Pearson Education.

Wright, P. 1984. *On Living in an Old Country: The National Past in Contemporary Britain.* London: Verso.

Yarwood, R. and Edwards, W. 1995. Voluntary Action in Rural Areas: the case of Neighbourhood Watch, *Journal of Rural Studies*, 11, 4, 447–59.

Yarwood, R. and Gardner, G. 2000. Fear of Crime, Culture and the Countryside, *Area*, 32, 4: 403–411.

Young, J. 1999. *The Exclusive Society.* London: Sage.

Young, J. 2007. *The Vertigo of Late Modernity.* London: Sage.

Index